W9-ATA-934

Coach Odle's Full Court Press

Jessica Rousselow-Winquist
Alan H. Winquist

Taylor University Press
Upland, Indiana

Copyright © 2001 by Jessica Rousselow-Winquist, Alan H. Winquist
Library of Congress Catalog Card Number: 2001 135977
ISBN# 0-9621187-7-X

Cover design by Steve Christensen

The front cover includes several items from the display case in the lobby of the Odle Gymnasium at Taylor University—

- A basketball used in the 1960 Olympics in Italy. The Chinese Olympic team signed the ball and presented it to Coach Odle.
- A game jersey with Chinese characters worn by Taylor University's All-American Forrest Jackson on the first Venture for Victory tour during the summer of 1952.
- A medallion from the Freedom's Foundation, Valley Forge, Pennsylvania with the inscription "Honoring Taylor University 'Venture for Victory' 1952." On the back of the medallion is the following inscription: "For outstanding achievement in bringing about a better understanding of the American way of life."
- A trophy including a replica of a basketball with the inscription: "Venture for Victory Don Odle Coach P.I. [Philippines] Japan Formosa Korea 47,000 miles, 450,000 people, W [won] 82 L [loss] 1".
- A basketball net—"Taylor's final goal in Maytag Gymnasium was scored through this net. The game a 74-70 triumph over Hanover [College], marked the close of 45 years of exciting competition in the former [Taylor University] gym."

Also pictured on the cover are two items owned by the Taylor University Archives—a Venture for Victory jersey in gold and purple, the colors of Taylor University; a decorative brass cup from Cambodia with an inscription in French "Federation Cambodgienne Basket-ball Cambodge Venture for Victory (USA) 1 août [August] 1963".

Not pictured on the cover and located in the lobby of the Odle Gym is a basketball used by the Japanese Olympic team in 1964 and presented to Coach Odle by Prince Takamatsu after a five game series with the Venture for Victory team. The Japanese team members signed their names on the basketball.

All rights reserved
Printed in the United States of America

TABLE OF CONTENTS

COACH ODLE'S FULL COURT PRESS

COACH ODLE'S FULL COURT PRESS

COACH ODLE'S FULL COURT PRESS

This VV logo was displayed on the 1962 team blazer.

PREFACE

I have often referred to Don Odle as "the father of sports evangelism." Obviously there were Christians in sports before Don Odle, and I am sure many used their athletic platform as a springboard for evangelism. But it was with the birth of Venture for Victory that organized attempts for the first time used competition and forthright witness as an outreach tool. It is doubtful that the concept would have been nearly as successful if it were not for the unique qualities possessed by this dynamo of personality and energy. Words like effervescent, irrepressible, affable and even unflappable are those used to describe Don. Those who know him best recognize that he is intense, focused and results oriented. He has sublimated his personal desires to accomplish goals. He is committed to a positive spirit of "can do" and has chosen to take the high road. He will not be negative, will not criticize and will not put others down. Don is a superb athlete, certainly above average in any sport he tried from basketball to golf. However, it is the combination of many qualities that makes the package work. He is a competitor but not at the expense of good humor. He likes to win but enjoys his own foibles and admires his opponent's abilities. Almost all of his humor is at his own expense. He never forgets that after all it is a game, and friendships and human relationships last long after the score is forgotten. He develops his players beyond the sport. Thoughtfulness, sportsmanship, courtesy, humor, respect and love for one another outrank winning or even teaching the fundamentals.

While playing in Asia against national teams with a bit of U.S. pride on the line, he never forgot that the real purpose was to represent Christ by exhibiting Christian character along with basketball skills. Few men possess the combination of qualities blended together with dedication, flexibility, grit and sacrifice to make such a program succeed. Don did it. For me, it will always be "hats off" to Don, one of the most unforgettable characters I have ever known," and to Bonnie who covered his tracks so all of us would admire him.

> Jay Kesler
> Chancellor, and former President
> Taylor University

Occasionally into one's life comes an individual whose enthusiasm for his faith and his profession is both admirable and contagious. As a freshman at Taylor University, I met such a person in Coach Don Odle.

His consistent witness for our Lord was evident in all phases of his life, including basketball, which was my passion at the time. When the call came to bring a team of college players to the Orient to play ball and share their faith in Christ, a concept unheard of at that time, "Coach" accepted the challenge. His willing obedience stood as a shining example of one's response to God's leading. Thus, the ministry of

COACH ODLE'S FULL COURT PRESS

Venture for Victory and what is now known as sports evangelism was born.

As a member of the 1957 Venture for Victory team, I am sure I shared many of the same opportunities as members of all other teams of this type. Foreign travel, people, places, foods, churches, basketball stadiums were all encounters far beyond the typical college life. Above all, my own faith was challenged and strengthened as a result of these experiences.

Because of Coach Odle's faithfulness to the apostle Paul's admonition to "become all things to all men...", my own experiences with Venture for Victory, as well as my four years at Taylor were the foundations for my own Christian growth. I consider it a privilege to have been a student and player of his, and he continues to be my mentor.

George Glass
Member 1957
Venture for Victory Team
Former track and field coach and
Athletic Director,
Taylor University

left to right—George Glass, Jay Kesler, Don Odle

COMMENTS AND ACKNOWLEDGEMENTS FROM AUTHORS

While we were researching our previous book entitled *God's Ordinary People: No Ordinary Heritage* written for Taylor University's 1996 sesquicentennial celebrations, the authors had several interesting conversations with Don and Bonnie Odle. We learned that Coach Odle had written an unpublished manuscript reviewing his life and accomplishments. After talking with several people about "Coach's" career, we realized there was a unique and significant story to be told about Don Odle and Taylor University, and the role this man and institution have played in the development of the worldwide Christian sports evangelistic movement. It is particularly appropriate to consider the impact and heritage of Venture for Victory (VV) at this time since 2002 will mark the 50th anniversary of this organization's birth. We approached Gene Rupp,

COACH ODLE'S FULL COURT PRESS

Taylor University's Vice President for Development, with the idea of doing additional research and eventually writing a book focusing on Venture for Victory. We are deeply grateful to Gene Rupp and Taylor University for encouraging us to proceed with the project.

The focus of this book is twofold. Primary attention is given to demonstrating Don Odle's role as the central figure in the unfolding early story of the sports evangelistic movement. In addition Venture for Victory and the Taylor University players and coaches who have been a part of VV and its successor organization known as Sports Ambassadors receive extensive discussion. We hope that former players from other universities and colleges participating in VV programs will understand and appreciate the objective of this book.

Perhaps it might appear unusual that two professors – an historian and a rhetorical critic – should be writing this book. However, the authors believe that their knowledge of historical and critical research methodologies have enabled them to write an objective book that provides fresh insights into the subject. This has been a fascinating topic for us and we have been enriched by having had the privilege of becoming acquainted through interviews with a number of outstanding committed Christians who know, love, respect, and admire Don and Bonnie Odle. Their stories and reminiscences have added texture and nuance to the Odle story, and have been a rich source of inspiration for the authors. Many of the extensive interviews we have conducted were recorded by permission and will become part of the Taylor University archival collection.

Coach Odle's Full Court Press required extensive interviewing in order to reconstruct past events as accurately as possible. Without the outstanding cooperation that we received from numerous people, this book could not have been written. We are very grateful to many people who have donated their time to be interviewed as well as those who allowed us to read their diaries, borrow their photographs, and look at memorabilia from their experiences with Venture for

Victory. Especially we want to thank Don Jacobsen for his insights, his priceless diary and photographs, and for reading part of our manuscript and offering us very helpful suggestions. We also wish to give special thanks to Jay Kesler and Dwight Jessup for reviewing parts of our work and for their encouragement. Norm Cook spent a considerable amount of time with us both in Winona Lake, Indiana, and at Taylor University in which he gave us valuable information about Don Odle and the early years of Venture for Victory. At Taylor University Norm was joined by his wife, Muriel. In addition, we want to thank the following people who allowed us to interview them either in person or by telephone: Don Callan, Clyde Cook, Ellsworth Culver, Barbara Davenport, Bob Davenport, Tim Diller, Ted Engstrom, Gary Friesen, George Glass, Don Granitz, Dick Hillis, Charles (Chuck) Holsinger, Roger Jenkinson, Jay Kesler, Jack King, Josephine Miller, Joe Romine, Bud Schaeffer, Eddie Waxer, Rev. Andrew Wingfield-Digby, and Ted Wright.

A number of people have contributed significant photographs. They include Norm Cook, Tim Diller, Gary Friesen, George Glass, Don Granitz, Chuck Holsinger, Roger Jenkinson, Jack King, Don Odle, Bud Schaeffer, and Larry Winterholter. We also wish to thank Janet Friesen for locating a number of valuable photographs and materials. We are grateful to the Indiana Basketball Hall of Fame for granting us permission to use the sketch appearing on page 8. We thank Bonnie Houser and Dan Bowell of the Taylor University Archives and Library for helping us with this project as well as the assistance of the Billy Graham Archives (Wheaton, Illinois), Wandering Wheels, and the Grace College Library and its director, Bill Darr. Copies of various Manila, Philippines newspapers were obtained at the New York Public Library. The sketch introducing Chapter 3 on page 62 appeared in an issue of *Look Magazine* entitled "Look Applauds." The photographs on pages 53 and 56 are used by permission of the Grace College Archives and OC International respectively.

COACH ODLE'S FULL COURT PRESS

Other people deserve special mention. Rev. and Mrs. J. Murray Marshall of Seattle, Washington suggested the book title and gave us important insights regarding the early development of the evangelistic movement following World War II. Our thanks to Bill Ringenberg for his constructive comments, and to Jay Kesler and George Glass for writing the Preface. Steve Messer and Thomas Jones have researched the October 30, 1954 football game between Taylor University and Fisk University, and we are greatful for their input. Special appreciation certainly goes to Arna Smith for her expert work in setting up the text for the publisher, to Jim Garringer for his outstanding photographic work, to Dan Jordan in locating a publisher, and to Steve Christensen for creating the eye catching cover design. Many other people gave us insights and advice, and we are most appreciative to all.

Finally the authors are deeply grateful to Don and Bonnie Odle. Not only did they show outstanding hospitality to the authors, but also they gave us a considerable amount of their time to be interviewed by sharing their memories, photographs and mementos. Without their cooperation this book could never have been written. Don's unpublished manuscript, *Taylor Made,* was a key resource for this book. It takes a long time for a book to be researched and written, and we appreciate their patience. Most of all we have been inspired by their love for the Lord and their consistent Christian witness. Thank you, Don and Bonnie, for sharing your inspiring lives with us and with those who will read *Coach Odle's Full Court Press.*

Jessica Rousselow-Winquist and
Alan H. Winquist

Note of clarificiation from the authors: In this book we are using the terms "East Asia" rather than "The Far East", or "Orient", and "Taiwan" rather than "Formosa."

INTRODUCTION

The post-World War II period saw significant changes in Protestant evangelical Christianity. Chief among these new developments was the creation of an exciting new approach to ministry—sports evangelism. The very first effort to connect athletics and evangelism was born in what seemed an unlikely place—a small evangelical college in America's heartland named Taylor University (TU). Fifty years ago, this innovative concept was developed through a cooperative effort in which three Christian institutions and organizations—Taylor University, Orient Crusades, and Youth for Christ—played key roles. The synergy created by combining their personnel and resources produced a new entity called Venture for Victory (VV) dedicated to the effort of Christian evangelism. *Coach Odle's Full Court Press* is the story of

1

this organization and its role in developing the concept of sports evangelism.

Winona Lake, Indiana was a crossroads of evangelicalism in the late 1940s and early 1950s. Taylor University located in Upland, Indiana was a two hour drive from the Winona Lake Conference Center, home of the Billy Sunday Tabernacle. Taylor faculty members, including Don and Bonnie Odle, regularly spent summers attending meetings held in the great tabernacle famous for its sawdust trail. Taylor students also came to Winona Lake to serve as counselors and staff members. Here evangelists such as Bob Pierce, many Taylor alumnae including Norm and Muriel Cook, and missionaries like Richard (Dick) Hillis, met to plan new strategies for carrying the message of Christianity to the world in the early days of the post-World War II era.

Organizations provide the bureaucratic structure that enables programs such as Venture for Victory to function, but it is the personnel working within these entities who put legs on new ideas. The men who organized and sustained Venture for Victory through the fifties and early sixties all possessed a cluster of personality traits that uniquely fitted them for this enterprise. A strong Christian commitment which included a belief in Christ's Great Commission to "Go into all the world and preach the gospel" provided the foundation on which they built. In addition to this deep conviction, they all had developed compassionate hearts for the people to whom they sought to minister. But conviction and compassion alone would not have been enough to birth this truly pioneer concept in evangelism. These men also needed to be willing to take risks as they entered the hitherto uncharted territory of sports evangelism. The success of their mission depended on cultivating the good will of political and business leaders in the countries with which they were involved. The ability to construct networks with a wide variety of people in East Asia was needed. A good sense of humor and the ability to laugh at one-

Introduction

self helped to create positive rapport with the Asian people. At the same time, athletic contests are about winning and losing, a fact that necessitated the cultivation of an appropriately competitive spirit in those who led and played on the Venture for Victory teams.

Several charismatic leaders had already emerged within Taylor University, Orient Crusades, and Youth for Christ, and they were now poised to work together to create a viable new program for Christian outreach in East Asia. Don Odle, Athletic Director and basketball coach at Taylor University, had earned a reputation in Indiana as a result of developing a very competitive athletic program in a relatively short period of time. Dick Hillis and Ellsworth Culver, co-founders of Orient Crusades, were laboring as evangelists in Taiwan. Billy Graham, Bob Pierce and Ted Engstrom, among others, were deeply involved in Youth for Christ work in the United States and other countries. Engstrom was to serve as the catalyst for the new venture bringing Hillis and Culver together with Odle. This was particularly fortuitous because while Hillis and Culver originated the idea of bringing a basketball team to play in Taiwan, they had no access to such a team. Odle had a heart for world wide evangelism but had never traveled outside of the United States and had not previously considered the possibility of taking a sports team to East Asia. He did, however, have a championship basketball team comprised of young men, many of whom also had a keen interest in missions.

A strategy of evangelism combined with sports emerged in the early 1950s. At this time the definition of a missionary was one who left her/his country of origin and went to live in a foreign land for an extended period of time. The assumption was that missionaries had to learn the language and establish connections within the new culture if they were to have an effective ministry. Since the idea of short term missionary workers was new, a major challenge faced by Odle and the Venture for Victory teams was to demonstrate the possibility of exerting a significant impact for Christ on the culture even though they came for a truncated period of time.

Odle's boundless enthusiasm for Taylor University made him a natural ambassador for this educational institution. He was an entertaining, effervescent speaker much sought after by churches and civic organizations. TU student musicians frequently accompanied Odle on these outreach ventures. "Coach" drew on these experiences in planning the first VV trip. One of the qualifications for being a member of a Venture for Victory team was the ability to sing or play a musical instrument and to address a large audience. The long intermission between the first and second halves of a basketball game provided an appropriate time for the players to present a program of music and testimonials. Out of these combined experiences, a unique evangelistic model was created. Brochures were printed with the American team member's pictures on the front. On the back was a section where an individual could indicate interest in enrolling in the Bible correspondence course. Local pastors and missionaries helped the VV players to distribute and collect these programs. After the game was over, interested audience members were invited to stay and hear how they could become followers of Christ.

While individual VV team members often talked and prayed with inquirers, it was the missionaries and pastors who had the responsibility to follow up with a potentially large number of people who made a commitment to follow Christ. The challenge for Orient Crusades was to develop a method for maintaining contact with these people. Orient Crusades found the Navigator Bible correspondence course translated into Chinese to be an effective way to meet this objective.

Coach Odle's Full Court Press is the story of the symbiotic relationship that developed between various career missionaries and the VV teams. Initially, missionaries who were affiliated with Orient Crusades and Youth for Christ were the ones who worked most closely with Odle. However, individuals affiliated with other mission organizations, most notably James and Lillian Dickson, also played a significant role in enlarging the ministry opportunities that were presented each summer to VV. It soon became evident to all concerned that this relationship was mutually beneficial. The presence of these vibrant, energetic, committed young sportsmen served to attract larger audiences for the Gospel than any single mission organization could otherwise have hoped to reach. During the two and a half months VV spent annually in East Asia, missionaries and the Christian message took center stage. At the same time, the young men did not spend all their time playing basketball. They learned what the life of a career missionary was really like. They witnessed first hand the social and political realities of the East Asian countries they visited. The horror of war was close at hand. They visited hospitals filled with wounded soldiers. They saw homeless, political refugees, orphaned, hungry children and abandoned lepers. Shortly after the Korean armistice was signed in 1953, VV went to Korea and experienced the absolute devastation that had been visited on that country. As a result of these experiences, a number of VV players became career missionaries with Orient Crusades and other similar organizations.

Coach Odle's Full Court Press is also the story of tensions and conflicting priorities. In the early 1950s the young Americans who joined VV teams were used to playing competitive basketball on their own home turf. They knew how the game was played. When they came to East Asia they discovered that basketball was the number one sport in several countries including the Philippines and Taiwan. However, they also learned that the rules were not always the ones they were used to and the referees were occasionally strongly biased in favor of the home team. The fans were dedicated to their teams and sometimes behaved in singularly unruly ways. Beginning with the very first 1952 team, VV played in a wide variety of places ranging from pick-up games in the urban barrios and rural villages to well publicized contests in major arenas in large cities. They played against military and college squads, and against both semi-professional and professional teams. They even played against the national Olympic teams in the Philippines and the Republic of China (Taiwan). Throughout the 1950s VV won nearly all their games, often by significant margins. However, in the early 1960s this situation was changing. The Asian players were developing greater expertise on the court. They fielded taller, stronger, more skillful teams. The desire to win remained strong with Odle and his men, and they still went home at the end of the summer with far more wins than losses. However, the losses increasingly came in the larger arenas when VV met the professional teams whose desire to win matched their own competitive spirit. Although Odle and VV never lost sight of their evangelistic mission, they found it tempting to place winning contests as a more important priority than in previous years.

Coach Odle's Full Court Press is the story of widening circles of influence. Venture for Victory is the very first organization to deliberately bring athletics and evangelism together in an international context. However, VV was only the beginning. Today there are hundreds of sports organizations sponsored by colleges, Christian youth groups and local churches whose mission is to take the Christian Gospel to many different parts of the world. Like VV, some of these groups focus on the fans. Others such as Athletes in Action, a division of Campus Crusade, and Fellowship of Christian Athletes, minister to athletes. Many of these groups were established by former VV players, and most of them continue to use the evangelistic model developed by Odle in the 1950s.

Introduction

DON ODLE
Worldwide ambassador of Indiana basketball

Chapter One

THE POWER OF ONE

The loss of innocence shaped the post-World War II generation of Americans. Suddenly, the nation found itself thrust onto the world stage, forced out of isolation by the millions of returning service men and women. Journalists and photographers stationed in the European and Pacific theatres were frequently in close proximity to the war and its aftermath. For the first time, their reports kept Americans abreast of the events of the war as it unfolded. A new awareness of global responsibility was born. Military leaders such as Dwight Eisenhower, Douglas MacArthur, George Marshall and George Patton captured America's imagination. Political leaders including Franklin Roosevelt, Winston Churchill and Harry Truman became regular guests in American living rooms through the miracle of radio.

COACH ODLE'S FULL COURT PRESS

The outpouring of appreciation for the returning GIs served to revitalize the American Dream. The GI Bill of Rights made college education affordable for the ordinary soldier. Taylor University was among the colleges benefiting from the GI Bill. Increased numbers of experienced, mature male students arrived on the campus. Many of these men were eager to broaden Taylor's athletic program by raising the level of intercollegiate competition and possibly introducing new sports. Don Odle became Taylor University's Athletic Director at a propitious moment. His vision for the athletic program coincided with the influx of GIs, and through a combination of political "savvy", skill in building networks and the courage to seize opportunities, he was able to put legs on new ideas.

Warm Ups and Drills

Don Odle was born on May 12, 1920 in Muncie, Indiana. The family home was near the Ball State University campus. Morton Pearl Odle, his father, was a farmer and painter who began a paint company in 1926. His mother was Rebecca Moriah Woodland. Don Odle was the youngest in a family of nine children. Odle recalls "there were so many of us around the table that I never had a chair to sit on. I would stand at the corner of the table and eat my meal."[1] The family had a garden, a cow and some chickens and he recalls that during his sixth and seventh years in grade school his lunch every day consisted of "a cold egg sandwich." At a very early age Odle became an entrepreneur buying candy bars for three cents each and selling them for five cents apiece to the city merchants. When he was only nine years old, he began selling newspapers on the street corner. Odle recalled that, "I had to learn to be aggressive and competitive because I was the smallest kid selling papers... and bigger kids tried to run me off my spot. I felt I had to stand up for my territorial rights."[2] The neighborhood in which Odle spent his childhood was far from calm. His family lived down the street from Harry Copeland, a member of John Dillinger's gang. When people asked Odle if he was scared living in these neighborhoods, tongue in cheek, he would retort, "Dillinger works as an Avon lady in my neighborhood."[3] The most money Odle ever made selling papers was the day that John Dillinger escaped from the prison in Crown Point, Indiana.

Odle's parents emphasized practical training rather than formal education. As soon as they reached the age of 16, Odle's siblings left school and took jobs, but Odle graduated from high school. The only printed materials Odle remembers in his childhood home were copies of *The Prairie Farmer* magazine and his mother's Bible.

The Odle family moved several times during his youth making it necessary for him to change schools six times between the sixth grade and high school graduation. These moves were precipitated by Morton Odle's entrepreneurial spirit. He would buy a house that needed renovation, fix it up, and resell it. Don Odle said, "I saw [in my father's example] that you needed to try things. It does not hurt to fail. What hurts is not trying."[4]

Given the family's emphasis on training for specific employment rather than obtaining formal education and the frequent moves, it is amazing that Odle graduated from Selma, Indiana High School in 1938 where he played on the baseball team, and was the leading scorer on the basketball team. In fact, he always had been involved in some type of athletic competition since junior high when he won the Muncie wrestling championship in his division having been undefeated for three years. Odle was short in stature—5'8", extremely fast, and had particular strength in his hands which he attributed to the fact that as a boy he was required to do many chores including milking cows. He had begun playing basketball on the streets and back lots of Muncie when he was in elementary school.

COACH ODLE'S FULL COURT PRESS

By the time he was in the fifth grade he had already begun developing some of the skills of ball handling and shooting which would make him an effective high school and college player. He was attending Garfield Elementary in Muncie and the boys were obliged to practice outside on crushed stone. Odle remembers "this taught us to make a good fake with one quick dribble and shoot since the ball usually wouldn't bounce twice on that loose stone." He and his young teammates also developed some crowd dazzling moves in those school yard games. They got a ball with sewn raised seams and they learned "to put such 'English' on that ball that if we hit the top corner just right, the ball would ricochet through the middle of the hoop" making the "lucky boys top dog for the day."[5] The Garfield Grade School basketball team played the preliminary game before the Wilson Junior High squad took the court, and Odle recalls, "this was the most breathtaking experience of our [young] career."[6] The Muncie Central Bearcats were Odle's boyhood heroes. He would go to school early every morning just so he could catch a glimpse of these high school basketball players walking through Heekin Park on their way to Muncie Central. According to Odle, "all the boys tried to imitate their shooting, passing, and dribbling antics."[7]

Although his athletic achievements continued to be outstanding in high school, his academic performance was less than stellar. Odle described himself this way: "When I graduated from high school I was not valedictorian, but Val-e-ridiculous."[8]

Following graduation from high school, Odle planned to matriculate at Ball State University in Muncie. However, an unusual set of circumstances

12

occurred which brought him to Taylor University in the fall of 1938. Mr. C. L. Arthur, a Redkey businessman and owner of Redkey Canneries, had loaned Taylor University a sum of money which the institution was unable to repay. Taylor arranged with Arthur to cover the debt by granting five scholarships to students of his choice. At that time, the Taylor coach was Jesse England who had previously coached in Redkey and was acquainted with Arthur. Arthur had seen Odle play basketball against the Redkey team and had been impressed with his ability. The latter suggested that England talk to Odle and see if he could be interested in coming to Taylor as one of the five scholarship recipients. England followed through with this suggestion and assured Odle that he would be able to try out for the varsity basketball team as a freshman, an opportunity that probably would not have been obtainable at Ball State.

Odle came to Taylor with a mere $50 in his savings account, a tuition scholarship and the promise of a job to earn his room and board. He did not own a suitcase, so he had packed all of his possessions except his sports coat in a paper shopping bag. His father drove him to campus in the family 1935 Chevrolet and let him out in front of McGee-Campbell-Wisconsin Dormitory. His father's parting words were, "Good luck, son. I hope you get along all right."[9] There was no freshman orientation program and Odle did not know anyone at Taylor except Coach England, but he recalls that "it wasn't long until I knew everyone on my floor and I'm sure there were several who wished that I hadn't arrived."[10] One of these people was Ted Engstrom whom Odle clearly remembers did not like him when they met the first week on Taylor campus.[11] Odle described himself as "cocky, aggressive, brash... a real 'hot dog' out to make an impression... with a vile, abominable tongue".[12]

One of the activities during the first week of school was a baseball game pitting the upper classmen against the freshmen. Odle was on the latter team and Engstrom played for the upper classmen. Before the game, Odle realized that he was the only player who did not have a pair of baseball spikes. In fact, he had never had spikes even though he had played three years of high school baseball and had been an outstanding hitter for his team. After the game Coach England located an old pair of baseball shoes which had been left behind by some former player. The spikes were too big, but England stuffed cotton in the toes and Odle wore them the entire season during his freshman year.[13]

Despite his negative feelings about Odle, Engstrom "took him on as a prayer project" and subsequently had a big influence on Odle's life.[14] Although Odle's parents had attended church when he was a small child, they had subsequently ceased to be involved. Consequently, Odle had no concept of what a Christian college was all about. He was mystified by such campus activities as prayer meetings and Bible studies. Odle recalls that the experience of adjustment was so difficult that he often "felt like an old maid in an unwed mother's home."[15] Not only did Odle find the religious atmosphere of the campus strange, but he was also intimidated by the rules governing social interaction. On his first day at Taylor he was told he would be required to wear a coat and tie to dinner. Entering the dining room he discovered that the students were assigned to tables seating six women and six men. The men were expected to seat the women and "Emily Post etiquette" was observed at all meals. Dining hall decorum was enforced by the "Junior Rules Committee." Odle found that "for a guy who could pig his food down with a shovel, this was quite an adjustment."[16]

As September moved on, Odle felt himself increasingly frustrated and tormented by this "fish out of water" feeling. That fall an evangelist named Dr. P.B. Smith came to campus to hold the annual revival meetings. On October 3, 1938, Odle decided to go to the altar to get his life straightened out. He recalls that he "spent about two hours on his knees" and several people including Olive May Draper, professor of mathematics and astronomy, and Ted Engstrom came to pray with him. Odle remembers that he "went back to the dorm that night and went to bed for the first time in his life with a clear conscience."[17] This experience was so overwhelming that Odle immediately began sharing his new found faith with the members of his family and his Muncie friends. Although his family was generally supportive, Odle discovered that not everyone understood his enthusiasm. Two of his closest high school friends rejected him and his conversion "built a wall between [him] and some of [his] brothers and sisters."[18]

Certainly his conversion was a profound experience, but it did not change Odle's basic personality. He was still impulsive, impudent, fun-loving, competitive, aggressive and a bit of a dare devil. Odle recounts one day in March during his freshman year he was walking back to the dormitory from the dining hall. There had been a spring snow storm followed by sunshine which had turned the landscape into slush. One of his friends called from the open dormitory window chiding him about his "lousy monopoly game" the night before. Odle picked up a handful of slushy snow, packed it into an ice ball and hurled it at his friend in the window. However, his friend was quicker than he was and slammed the window shut. The ice ball hit the glass, breaking it. The next day Odle was summoned into Dean George Fenstermacher's office where he was reminded that the Dean's patience was wearing thin "with some of [Odle's] stupid escapades" and Odle was ordered to pay for the broken window.[19]

On another occasion Odle's cockiness nearly got him into very serious trouble. At that time the McGee side of the dormitory housed women and men lived on the Campbell side. One evening after dinner a number of women came out on their third floor balcony and several men appeared on the other side of the balcony. They were laughing, singing and talking loudly back and forth when Odle decided to take the limelight. He did a handstand on the balcony railing and then dangerously began to walk to the other end on his hands. Midway across he lost control and fell about 35 feet to the ground. He landed on his back between a sidewalk and a cement abutment. Girls screamed and fainted because they thought he had been killed, and a doctor was summoned to check for broken bones. Miraculously, Odle remained conscious and sustained no serious injury, but the next day he was so stiff and sore that he had a hard time walking to class.[20] One of the people who witnessed Odle's fall was Josephine Erler who worked in the business office. Remembering the event she said, "he got right back up there and did the handstand again just to prove he could!"[21]

Towards the end of the year the campus community was involved in what was called "clean up day." The students were rambunctious, and Odle "did a couple of stupid things like throwing water on the senior class president." Two seniors, Engstrom and Charles Smith, grabbed Odle shouting "Let's throw him in the river!" They put him in the back seat of a car and drove to the Mississinewa. Six carloads of students followed to watch the spectacle of Odle getting some of his own medicine. Odle described what happened when they got to the river bank.

> I jerked loose from Engstrom and Smith, put my arms around both of them; and we all three tumbled down the river bank into the water together... As we hit, I swam underneath the water for several feet and then across the river. All of our clothes were soaked and our shoes were full of water... There was no way they could catch me on the other side of the river, so I felt that I won the fight in the end.[22]

Academics continued to be an area where Odle struggled. He quips, "Since I didn't have any more sense of direction than an eggbeater, my academics were secondary and I had no idea of a major."[23] One class in which this was particularly evident

16

was "Harmony of the Gospels", taught by Dr. Jasper Abraham Huffman. Odle says that at the time he did not know the difference between the Old and New Testaments and was totally unprepared for any Bible class. He missed every question on the first ten point quiz. He remembers that one question on the quiz was "Who was John the Baptist?" His answer was that he was a Baptist minister. Another question asked "Why are the first four books of the New Testament called the Harmony of the Gospels?" His answer was, "all the authors were singers." As the class progressed he did begin to improve, but when it came to the final exam he failed. He prepared himself for a failing grade in the course, but two of his friends interceded for him with Huffman explaining that Odle was a new Christian and was just beginning to read the Bible. Huffman gave him a C-, and Odle says, this was a grade "that changed the course of [his] life" because it allowed him to remain at Taylor University where he majored in history and education.[24]

Odle had come to Taylor primarily because he had been promised an opportunity to play varsity ball immediately. He joined about twenty-five other Taylor men including a number of returning players in trying out for the basketball team in the fall of 1938. Because of his lack of height, his chances of being selected did not appear very good. However, Odle's assessment of this apparent liability shows his spunky determination. "Where I came from they measured a man from the ears up."[25] At first he was not chosen to be on the top ten. However, by Thanksgiving he was "a bench warmer just trying to get more playing time" and by Christmas he was playing on the varsity and scoring a few points in each game. It turned out to be a very successful season for Odle. The 1939 *Gem* reported that "Pidge" (a nickname for Odle) combined speed and faking to be high scorer his first season. He was a crack shot under the basket and was generally there when needed.[26] When asked about the origin of the nickname, Odle quipped, "My toes got sleepy so they turned in!" In addition to playing basketball that year, Odle was also a shortstop on the baseball team and was a pole vaulter.

Intercollegiate athletics was still in the early stages of development during Odle's undergraduate years. Maytag Gymnasium had been substantially completed and was dedicated in 1930. In October 1932 the Board of Trustees had passed a resolution permitting the entry of Taylor into the realm of intercollegiate competition.[27] This did not actually begin until the 1933-34 school year, and there were still relatively few events scheduled in basketball, baseball and track. The University had employed A. H. Cornwell to be Director of Athletics in 1931, and one of the first things he did was to create the "T" club. During his tenure he began the transition from an institution based athletic program to an intercollegiate one. During the first season of competition, the Taylor Trojans won ten and lost five of their basketball games. However, this winning record was not again repeated in subsequent seasons. For the next three years (1934-37) the Trojans could not find their way back to the plus side of the ledger winning only six of twenty, two of sixteen and three of seventeen contests.[28]

Odle's student days at Taylor University

The program was still undergoing growing pains during Odle's years as a student. However, he was able to contribute significantly to the development of both the basketball and baseball programs. During his sophomore year Odle led Taylor's basketball team in scoring. He became known for his "faking and his continuous drive, as well as his accurate shooting."[29] Odle's junior year was marked by increasing notoriety as he continued to lead the Trojans in scoring while honing his now near legendary skills.[30] "Pidge was one of the co-captains and for the fourth consecutive year has led the Taylor scoring—this year being second in the state competition. His speed, faking and accurate shooting will always be remembered."[31]

One particularly memorable basketball game occurred in November of Odle's junior year. It was the first game of the season pitting the Trojans against Concordia College, and it turned out to be a "barn burner". Odle was the outstanding scorer, netting thirty points which broke the previous record of 29 held by Art Howard, a 1938 graduate and co-founder of the Taylor University Gates-Howard award for outstanding athletic achievement.[32] Coincidentally, this was also the first time a freshman coed, Bonnie Weaver, was in the bleachers.[33]

Odle had first become aware of Weaver when he saw her photograph in her brother Jack's room. At the time, Don was dating another young lady, but when he saw this photograph, he decided on the spot that this girl was destined to be his. Bonnie met Don for the first time when she came to visit her brother. She recalls only that Jack introduced her to "this guy who was wearing big clodhopper shoes!"[34] The following year Bonnie matriculated at Taylor. Don was acting as a "bellhop" assigned to help carry the women's bags to their rooms. He knew that the Weavers were coming that afternoon and he kept a sharp lookout for their Chrysler. When she arrived, he made sure he was the one to carry her bags, and he lost no time asking her if he could walk her to the post office after dinner— one of the few legitimate times when Taylor men and women were allowed to be together on campus. This "post office date" was the beginning of their three year courtship which culminated in their marriage on July 8, 1944.

Bonnie Weaver was born January 6, 1922 in Tiger Mountain, Oklahoma, the second child of Fred and Cleo Beekman Weaver. Fred Weaver had attended Marion Normal School and had earned a teacher's certificate from Muncie Normal School. Cleo Beekman lived with her parents and a sister on a farm south of the Taylor campus, and attended some classes at Taylor but did not graduate. While she was on campus she also worked as a secretary to Dr. Burt Ayres. Beekman married Weaver in 1919, and for a short time the young couple resided in Indiana where Fred taught school. Then they moved to Oklahoma to join Fred's father and brother in the oil fields. Fred also obtained a teaching job in a school for Native American children.

In 1923, the Weaver family returned to Indiana, and Fred Weaver enrolled in classes at Ball State University where he completed his B.A. degree with a major in mathematics. He subsequently completed his M.A. at Butler University and pursued a career in secondary teaching and administration in the Anderson and Indianapolis school systems. Needless to say education was highly valued in the Weaver home and both Jack and Bonnie were encouraged to pursue a college education. Bonnie said of her father, "He was a great inspiration to me. He loved poetry and encouraged me a great deal in my studies."[35]

Weaver's encouragement of his daughter yielded significant results. She attended Anderson High School where there were 465 students in her class. During her senior year she was elected class president and received an award from the Daughters of the American Revolution as the outstanding girl in her high school. Bonnie said that her high school experience prepared her exceptionally well to do college work. She had applied to Indiana University and had been granted a scholarship, but she knew that her parents would be happier if she went to Taylor with her brother. [36]

The Power of One

Don took full advantage of his first "post office date" with Bonnie, finding other opportunities to be with her. When she spent her evenings working and studying in the library, he would go there toward closing time and then walk her back to the residence hall even though this was stretching Taylor's rules of decorum. He quips "while other students went to the library to check out books, he went to check out the librarian!"[37] Bonnie said "it was never boring to have a date with this guy. He thought of many fun and interesting things to do even though this some-times led to some embar-rassing moments for her." On one occasion they were eating together in the dining room. The jello was particularly rubbery and Don could not resist playing the clown. He took some of it and bounced it off his biceps to dem-onstrate its inedible con-sistency. When one of the other students told him to grow up, Don promptly threw a lump of jello at the guy. This was not approved dining room decorum and a member of the "junior rules committee" descended on him. As a punishment for his behavior, Odle was assigned to sit at the faculty table for the next two weeks, a fate worse than death to a student like him.[38]

Don and Bonne Odle

The couple often double dated and on some of these occasions they would go to nearby Marion to watch two local high school teams, the Marion Giants and the Muncie Bearcats, battle it out on the football field. Don recalls one memorable evening. Bonnie was wearing a "glamorous black fur coat that she had received as a high school graduation gift from her mother." The other girl in the foursome was Betty Ladd, Grant County's "tomato queen". Don teased her mercilessly about "how many tomatoes she ate, or how many quarts she canned to get that award!" The evening was filled with "joking, laughing and unshackled hilarity."[39]

On at least one occasion the couple got into some fairly serious trouble. It was Bonnie's nineteenth birthday, and they requested permission to go to Marion for a special dinner and movie date with another couple. Their request was denied, but they decided to go anyway. When they returned, they were caught and all dates and privileges were suspended for one week. [40]

Even though they came from very different backgrounds, Don and Bonnie shared some important common values. Bonnie stated, "Don was a Christian before I was. I was a member of the church and a good girl. My issues were different from Don's but they were just as important to God." She went forward during the fall revival of her freshman year just as he had done. [41] If his Christianity influenced her in a positive direction, her commitment to academics did the same for him. He said, "she had academic ambitions that were absolutely foreign in my background. She went to the library every night and I was the rook champion!" As their relationship developed his grades improved. He recounts how he answered a question in Professor James Charbonnier's economics class which "astounded" that professor. After class, some of his friends asked him how he knew so much and Odle replied, "I really didn't know all those technical terms but I knew I could dazzle him with my footwork!" [42]

Getting In The Game

The 1941-42 year was marked by several important events for Odle. He had been playing baseball in various semi-professional and professional leagues around Indiana since graduating from high school. He had also played on Taylor's team and had earned an enviable .500 batting average. In the spring of 1942

The Power of One

prior to his graduation he received a letter from the Cincinnati Reds organization inviting him to come to spring training in Florida. After consulting with President Robert L. Stuart and Dean Earland Ritchie, it was decided that Odle should accept the invitation. The Reds sent him a train ticket and meal money, and the Taylor student body gave him a spectacular send off. Odle wrote of this experience, "We had three games against the parent club. I felt that my hitting and throwing were very good, but I had a difficult time fielding balls off the sand infield."[43]

Senior year at Taylor

During the time he was in Florida he received a letter from his draft board ordering him to report to Fort Benjamin Harrison in thirty days. When he returned to Indiana, Odle encountered a Marine recruiter who persuaded him to sign with the Corps with the promise that he would be allowed to finish college and would then have the opportunity to attend officer candidate school. Shortly after graduation in 1942 Odle reported to Quantico, Virginia to begin basic training. Odle loved the military life with its emphasis on physical activity and competition, but he was profoundly shocked when it was discovered that he had a "hernia and a gimpy knee" which would disqualify him from Officer's Candidate School. Odle headed home for Indiana deeply disappointed, expecting to be called by the Army. However, the local draft board had filled its quota and he was told to get a job. The draft board would call if he was needed. Odle still owed Taylor University $146 so he decided to take a teaching job at Union Township School.

Although Odle remained at Union Township for only half a year, he had a profound effect on its students and faculty. Odle capitalized on his marine training. First he organized military classes for both boys and girls where he taught them the requirements for the armed services. He instructed them in different types of marching commands and gave information about what to expect if they joined one of the branches of the military. He also used his position to create opportunities to evangelize, organizing the Youth Prayer League which met on Tuesday evenings for singing, testimonies and worship. In March 1943 Odle took a group of his students to Youth Conference at Taylor where a number of them went forward.[44] Union Township was also Odle's first coaching experience. He described the gym as one of the smallest he had ever seen. "It was 40' x 60' with the goals at the end lines against the walls. The ceiling was the top of the backboard so that you couldn't shoot beyond the free throw lanes."[45] There were only about fifty students in the entire school, scarcely enough to field a basketball team. Resources of every kind were meager.

Odle recalls a particularly significant incident after Union Township had just lost a game to Greentown. Odle and the team were in the locker room when the principal came in and began berating one of the players. For some reason, this young man responded by accusing the principal of stealing money from the athletic department. Such insolence was intolerable, and the principal hit the student in the face breaking his glasses. Odle reacted instinctively, grabbing the principal and shoving him out the door. "Coach" went home that night dejected thinking he would be fired for insubordination. Much to Odle's amazement, the principal was fired and he was offered the job![46]

Odle did not accept the job as principal. Instead, he signed a contract to coach at Frankton High School beginning in September 1943. Frankton was close to Anderson where Bonnie Weaver's parents lived. Don and Bonnie had become engaged at Christmas 1942, and she came to Anderson most weekends when Odle's team was playing. She became a good friend to the cheerleaders who looked up to her as a role model. After their marriage in the summer of 1944, the Odles returned to Frankton where Don worked with the YMCA as a Physical Director and Bonnie worked as a Recreation Director in Shadyside Park in Anderson. In the fall, Bonnie joined the faculty at Frankton High as an English teacher. They continued to be deeply involved in the lives of their students holding a Bible study during the noon hours where many students responded positively to the message of the Gospel.[47] In order to supplement their income, Odle played on a professional basketball team called the Anderson Packers. The sportswriter for the *Anderson Herald* described Odle as "one of the finest basketball players... with an array of feinting stances and ball handling techniques that provide the fans great viewing pleasure. The small but mighty former Taylor University star continually keeps the other team guessing with his amazing footwork and brilliant basketball eye."[48]

Wedding day — summer 1944

In the summer of 1945, with the encouragement of Bonnie's parents, the Odles enrolled at Indiana University in order to begin work on their masters degrees. Odle wanted to discover if, given the circumstances of his background and his late academic "blooming", he could be successful at the graduate level. He found that he could. Most of his grades were "As" and "Bs" and in mid-July he received a letter notifying him that he had been elected to candidacy for membership in Phi Delta Kappa, a national fraternity for education majors.[49] During the summer at Indiana University Odle met many people involved in secondary education resulting in three offers for coaching positions by the end of the summer. He and Bonnie decided that the job in Aurora, Indiana was the most promising, and in the fall they moved to that community where Don took up his duties as athletic director and coach of the football, basketball and baseball teams. In addition to teaching in the high school, Odle developed a community recreation program for the children. It was at this time that he also began to be actively involved in such organizations as Rotary, and he continued to play basketball and softball with the Aurora Merchants.[50]

Going For The Goal

In the spring of 1947 Odle received a telephone call from Dr. Clyde Meredith, Taylor University's President, offering him the job of athletic director and coach. Even though the move meant a substantial salary cut, Odle was certain this was God's will, and he, Bonnie and David, who had been born in 1946, moved to Upland.[51] In the 1940s, Taylor University was a small struggling institution. Its enrollments had declined to 159 students during the 1944-45 academic year. However, after the war, this trend was reversed and the enrollments steadily rose from 231 in 1945-6 to 613 in 1949-50. Along with other faculty members, Odle was determined to develop programs that would attract increased numbers of students to the University.

The salary was not only less than in Aurora; the workload was also heavier. Odle was the Athletic Director, coached basketball and baseball and taught a full load of classes in a wide variety of physical education subjects. He was also asked to teach a class in U.S. History with 93 students enrolled. This was the post-World War II era and the GIs were returning to the classroom to complete interrupted degrees or begin new ones. Although Taylor was attempting to deal with this influx of students, due to financial constraints it was unable to hire additional faculty. Odle said that though he had majored in physical education and history and enjoyed teaching the U.S. history class, he was not prepared to do this with all his other responsibilities. Odle gave this account of just one experience from the U.S. History class which illustrates the difficulties he encountered maintaining his schedule of coaching and teaching.

> One Tuesday night I drove over three hours to Hanover College to scout their basketball team. I didn't get back until long after midnight and overslept the next morning. I remember looking at my clock and seeing it was 7:50—the class started at 8:00. You can imagine how I scurried to get dressed and be in front of that class before they walked out on me... I rushed in the door just in time, and as I walked on to the platform where my lecture would take place, some of my athletes who were seated in the front row started whispering, 'Coach, your fly, your fly!' I looked down and saw that my shirttail was hanging out of my pant zipper... I decided to open the class with a prayer, thinking that everyone would close their eyes ... As I started to pray, I opened my eyes to discover that all the students were watching me zip up my pants while trying to pray. It was hilarious. Both the boys and the girls in the class started to giggle. When I finally stood up to lecture, it was impossible. I had to dismiss the class. The atmosphere, the humor, the embarrassment, and the sneaky giggles were more than I could handle.[52]

One of Odle's great strengths is his ability to communicate to a wide range of people in a variety of settings including the classroom. He is the master of the "one liner" and uses it shamelessly. One time he was teaching a high school class at Frankton and afterwards the principal's daughter came up to tell him that she liked the class but she did not like the jokes he sometimes made about Bonnie.[53] Even though his "one liners" got him into difficulty from time to time, he seemingly could not resist coining them. One of his favorite classes to teach was entitled "Minor Sports." He liked to begin the class by saying, "Bowling is not down my alley, tennis is not my racquet, golf tees me off, wrestling gets me down. I even tried parachuting, but nothing opened up. Even though I personally have not had a lot of successes in these sports, we are going to have a lot of fun in this class."[54]

In addition to his ability to catch and maintain student attention through his sometimes outrageous sense of humor, Odle was also an innovative and creative teacher. His classes were student centered, especially the class called Community Recreation. He began the class by defining recreation as "do[ing] what you want to do when you don't have to do it," and went on to say "if you don't enjoy this class, your professor has failed."[55] Odle designed many interesting experiences for the students including exposing them to the possibilities of recreation in a variety of settings including a retirement center and prisons. He also introduced them to people who were physically challenged but needed recreational opportunities. He took the class to the Mississinewa River to learn about camping. Everyone was required to cook and eat their own food. Odle observed that "no one got sick!" The capstone assignment in the course was to put on a county fair for the community in Maytag Gym. Every student was responsible for building a booth and working in it on the night of the fair. The sky was the limit in terms of utilizing their creative inspirations in developing ideas for booths. Some people probably thought that Maytag would never survive the invasion of chickens, ducks, goats, cows, pigs, colts and peacocks which was a part of the fair. However, the event was always a huge success drawing as many as 1000 people. It was also a terrific learning environment for those who participated in its production.[56]

Odle's innovative talents were utilized on the playing field as well as in the classroom. When he was a student at Taylor, Odle felt that the school needed football to create a truly collegiate atmosphere on campus and dispel the image of Taylor as a "preacher factory." As a faculty member, he was in a position to do something about the lack of football and he immediately set out to introduce the sport to the University. Odle has a strong, apparently innate, sense of the political, and he set out to enlist the support of the key people who could help him achieve his goal. Gilbert Dodd chaired the Physical Education Department, and his support was vital. Dodd joined Odle in making a presentation to the Taylor faculty recommending the addition of football. They faced some formidable opposition from those members of the faculty and administration who believed this sport was inappropriate for a Christian college. Those who opposed the idea included such Taylor stalwarts as Dr. Burt Ayres, Vice President of the University and Professor of Philosophy and Dr. Jasper A. Huffman, chairman of the Division of Bible. Nevertheless, the William Taylor Foundation, at the time the governing body of the school, approved the addition of football and in the spring of 1948 Odle held a ten day spring training and arranged a schedule of eight games for the following fall.

Football at Taylor got off to a somewhat inauspicious start. The University had hired a coach, but in the fall he decided not to come. This meant that Odle was faced with a difficult decision. Either he would have to abandon his idea to introduce the sport or he would have to coach the team. Odle said, "I was totally unprepared to coach football... but the decision was made on the premise of what was best for Taylor."[57] The problems he faced in beginning this program were indeed daunting and someone with a different personality might have found them insurmountable. He had virtually no budget. His players had no proper equipment or uniforms, and Odle had to appeal to sporting goods stores for any samples or mark downs they might be willing to donate. There was no proper playing field on the campus, no goal posts, no trainers or assistants of any kind. Half of the players who came out had never been on a football field before and did not even know how to put on the uniforms.

They played their eight games against such colleges as Anderson, Manchester, Huntington, Earlham, Canterbury (no longer in existence) and Hillsdale, and went down to defeat in every contest. The day after they lost the last game they were scheduled to appear in chapel. When they marched in to take their places on the platform the faculty and student body gave them a standing ovation. In fact, support for the new program seems to have been extremely high on the campus. The 1949 *Gem*, the school's yearbook, devoted a six-page spread including pictures of the football team. There was also an essay about the value of Taylor's decision to field a football team. Football was portrayed as having brought Taylor into "a higher level" of athletic competition. It was described as capable of building "Christian character" and "preparing the body for physical service." The writer acknowledged that Odle had a very tough

1949 football at Taylor University

The Power of One

assignment since he was "both the line and backfield coach." Nevertheless, "Coach Odle was able to give the squad excellent advice and training." The *Gem* writer summed up the first season as follows:

> This year Taylor's Trojans took a severe trouncing, but the players have the satisfaction of having brought one of the biggest gains to Taylor's athletic department in the last one hundred and two years. ...every week the players showed consistent team spirit and conducted themselves on the playing field as Christian athletes.[58]

Coaching athletic teams at the collegiate level does present myriad challenges and a wide variety of experiences. In Odle's words, "it seemed to me that in coaching you could be on the mountain-top one day, or lower than a mud hole at the bottom of a lake on another."[59] The first year of Taylor football must have provided moments "at the bottom of the lake" for Odle. He wrote, "we were out-coached and out-scored. I do believe in all out effort to accomplish our goals. That is what Taylor's first football team represented to me... football to me represents a lot about life. I guess that's why I enjoyed and endured."[60] However, as athletic director, Odle recognized that he could not carry the growing program by himself. In the fall of 1949 Odle hired Paul Williams as football coach. The addition of Williams had a clear payoff as the team won 4, lost 3 and tied 2, a record which far exceeded the expectations of even the most ardent supporters.[61]

If the first year of football sent Odle to the "bottom of the lake", his baseball and basketball teams were clearly taking him to the "mountain top". The first season with Odle at the helm was "one of the most successful in years for the varsity basketball squad." Twenty games were played with the team winning eleven contests including six of nine home games.[62] The next season was slightly better—12 wins and 8 losses. According to the *Gem*, "Close coordination of all players on the varsity gave a scoring combination which a majority of our opponents were unable to match... the scoring was evenly distributed among three or four players... Coach Odle molded a team that developed increasing smoothness."[63] The following year was Taylor's first as a member of the Hoosier Conference, and the Trojans clearly demonstrated that they were up to the challenges posed by the other Conference teams, Hanover, Anderson, Manchester, Franklin, Earlham, Indiana Central and Rose Polytechnic Institute. They played a total of 27 games and won six of their ten conference starts. Their record for the season was 19 wins and 8 defeats, a substantial improvement over the previous years. Three of the team members—Oral Ross, Norm Wilhelmi and Ted Wright—surpassed Odle's own career record of 323 points. The *Gem* declared this to be "one of the best teams ever to take the floor for Taylor."[64]

As a result of this steady growth and improvement, Dr. Ronald Jones, head of the Division of Education and Psychology and chair of the Athletic Committee, urged Odle to consider taking his basketball team to California to play against colleges beyond the Hoosier Conference. At first, Odle was dubious about the suggestion. He remembers asking Jones, "Do we hitchhike, walk, or how do we get there and where does the money come from?"[65] However, one of Odle's characteristics is that he is willing to try almost any reasonable suggestion even in the face of apparently unfavorable circumstances.

It often takes more than one person to bring an idea to fruition. In this case, Jones created the concept but Odle seized the opportunity and implemented the program. It was decided that the team would play these games immediately after Christmas 1949. The first problem was that of transportation, and Odle turned to Jones and others for help in finding a solution. It was finally decided to take Jones' car. Odle's brother, Orville who was nicknamed "double ought" drove a second car while Selah Wright, father of one of the players, Ted Wright, drove the third.[66] Having secured adequate transportation, Odle turned his attention to planning. Using his networking ability to advantage, he began calling alumni in the Far West asking them to help with arrangements and inquiring about the possibility of holding meetings in their churches. Within a relatively short time an itinerary had been arranged. The first game would be played in New Mexico, Highlands University, Las Vegas, New Mexico followed by Phoenix College in Tempe, Arizona, California Polytechnic State University (Cal Poly) in San Luis Obispo, Pasadena Junior College in Pasadena, and Westmont College in Santa Barbara. The problem of financing the trip demanded considerable negotiation on Odle's part. He received guarantees of $100 or $200 in gate receipts from each of the five colleges. He also obtained some housing in their dormitories and permission to eat at their school cafeterias. In addition, Odle arranged five speaking engagements for himself along the way. The gate receipts were used to pay for the gas and Odle's honoraria provided a small meal stipend of $1.00 a day for dinner and .75¢ for lunch for each player.[67]

The team was very successful, winning four of the five contests losing only to Cal Poly. The Trojans compiled 325 points on the trip for an average of 65 per game. One victory posed an interesting ethical dilemma. It was a very tight game against Highlands University. On the last play a Taylor netman stole the ball and a foul should have been called against him. However, the referee let the play continue. Taylor went on to score the winning basket, and the score at the end was 72-67. The opposing coach was justifiably irate at this "lousy call." The next night at Phoenix College Taylor squeaked by with a three-point win, 64-61. The game against Cal Poly was lost by a wide margin, 62-41. Odle said, "We arrived just two hours before the basketball game, stretched our legs and played terribly. We had left our basketball skills somewhere between Las Vegas and San Luis Obispo."[68] Taylor defeated Pasadena Junior College 67-50 and Westmont 81-54.

COACH ODLE'S FULL COURT PRESS

The drive home was extremely difficult. They drove all the way from Albuquerque, New Mexico to Upland through ice and snow. Upon arrival back home, Odle faced some criticism from faculty members who thought he was risking the lives of students unnecessarily for the sake of an overly ambitious schedule. Summing up the experience Odle wrote,

> When we finally arrived back in Upland, I was a basket case. I had had the responsibility of getting those student athletes to California and back in ten days... We learned a lot. We received a lot of favorable publicity. The trip attracted some other athletes to Taylor, and new vision had been confirmed about Taylor's athletic future.[69]

As a result of the successful California trip, Odle again took his Trojans "on the road" over Christmas break in 1950. This time they headed to the eastern seaboard where they first played a winning game against Harpur College in Binghamton New York (82-56), followed by Hofstra College on Long Island (57-51), University of Bridgeport Connecticut (86-78), and St. Michael's College, Burlington, Vermont (80-91). Shortly after the team left Upland they encountered their first problem in Celina, Ohio where because of icy conditions the lead car had difficulty stopping at a stop sign and slid into the car ahead. The Binghamton Press sportswriter headlined his article "Snow, Auto Crash, Harpur Fail to Stop Taylor."[70] Team member Ted Wright had several additional recollections of the trip. He recalled a second automobile accident in upstate New York toward the end of the tour. Wright remembers Odle's "lead foot" as he drove the leading car. The other drivers were constantly attempting to keep up the pace "Coach" set. Odle judged the game in Burlington to be their toughest contest on this trip. The opposition had a definite height advantage and the Trojans were suffering from sleep deprivation at this point in the trip. Wright recalls that initially the Trojans were behind 22-0 when he decided to begin using his famous hook shots which got them back into the game.[71] The final game of the series was played at Hartwick College where its team was coached by Tom Green, Odle's long time friend. Odle character-ized Hartwick as "a formidable foe", but at the final buzzer Taylor emerged victorious, 71-67.[72]

In December, 1951 Odle led the Trojan basketball team to Louisiana and Texas. The Taylor netters had just won the Hoosier Conference Tournament, the star being Ted Wright. In addition to Wright, the team starters included Howard Habegger, Carl Honaker, Forrest Jackson and John Bragg. John Nelson, Ron Morris and Ken Wright were also on the team. The first game was played against McNeese State University in Lake Charles, Louisiana. The score was 72-65 with Taylor on the short end. The team did not do as well on this southern swing as on previous trips. Their record was 2-3, winning against Southwestern Louisiana Institute in Lafayette and McMurry State in Abilene. In addition to losing to McNeese, the Trojans dropped two games to an army base team in San Antonio.[73]

The early fifties were the high point of Odle's basketball coaching career. The *Gem* declared, "The 1950-51 basketball season at Taylor was the most successful in the history of the school."[74] That year the Trojans won twenty-one games and lost only seven. They scored a total of 2214 points, an average of 79 per game, placing them fourth among the small col-leges nationally.[75] Over five hundred schools were in the National Association of Intercollegiate Athletics (NAIA) and of the top four, three were in Indiana—Indiana State number one, Evansville number two and Taylor number four. Two individual scoring records were set that year as Ted Wright netted 34 points in a single game, and Norm Wilhelmi "burned up the net" for a total of 392 points during the season.[76] The victory which brought the house down occurred in post season play during the opening round of the National Association of Intercollegiate Basketball (NAIB) Tournament. Taylor met and defeated Indiana

Central, a school that had beaten the Trojans twenty-seven times in as many starts. Taylor fan's jubilation was not even dampened by the fact that they lost the final round of the tournament to Evansville; the Trojans had won a great "moral victory."[77] The 1951-52 cagers ended the season with a record 21 wins and 4 losses. During the season Indiana Central went down to defeat three times against the Trojans. A particularly sweet victory that season was the two point win over Wheaton; the Trojans had lost to the Crusaders by one point the previous season.[78] It was during this time that Odle led the Trojans to two Hoosier Conference titles in 1951-52 and 1952-53.

Those glory days brought increased prestige and attention to the athletic department and to Taylor. For example, the *Gem* reported that the 1952-53 season had been "the toughest in Taylor history", but "they won the ones they had to" and finished with an overall record of 15-9 taking the Hoosier Conference Crown home for the second year in a row.[79] Even though their win-loss record does not look as impressive as the preceding two years, the team was still win-

1952-53 Taylor basketball team

ning honors. The most lauded player was Forrest (Jack) Jackson, the junior center from Gary, Indiana. Jackson smashed the Taylor scoring record in a spectacular way—he scored 63 points in the game against Huntington. This game also saw the Trojans set a new single game total of 115 points against the opposition's 59. At the end of the season, Jackson was honored for being among the top five scorers in the nation. Honors came to Odle as well as to his players as he was voted Net Coach of the Year in the Hoosier College Conference. By the end of the season Odle had also passed the "100 win hurdle" in his college coaching career.[80] However, in coaching, life on the mountain peaks cannot be sustained indefinitely and the 1954-55 season proved to be disappointing. The overall record for the team was 7-16 and the Trojans finished sixth in the Conference.

Nevertheless fan loyalty remained strong as witnessed by the *Gem*. The fans will always remember the spectacular battles waged by the Trojans. Although Taylor's basketball season was on the losing side of the ledger, the young squad showed lots of promise for the coming year. The team would also be bolstered the following season by the return of some outstanding servicemen.[81]

If basketball is Odle's first love, baseball is surely his second. His return to Taylor in 1947 signaled a new era for this sport. According to the 1949 *Gem*, "At one time an interclass sport on our campus, baseball now assumes a major place in the Department of Physical Education. Now Taylor's prowess on the baseball diamond is known by colleagues throughout the Midwest."[82] During his first few years as Taylor's Athletic Director Odle coached both basketball and baseball. By 1950 the Trojans had tied with Manchester to win their first conference championship. The 1951 season was somewhat disappointing as the baseball team finished with a record of 8 wins and 6 losses.[83] The "bright spots" in the 1952 season were two shutout games, one against Indiana Central and the other against

COACH ODLE'S FULL COURT PRESS

Wheaton.[84] In 1953 Odle relinquished coaching responsibilities for the team to Don Granitz who had played for Taylor during his four years as an undergraduate.

Through both the halcyon days and the disappointing times Odle gradually evolved his philosophy of coaching based on the three rules he posted in the dressing rooms: "#1–Hard Work, #2–Hard Work, #3–Hard Work." While he believed in discipline and made it clear to his players that there was "only one coach", he also understood a great deal about human psychology and motivation. He wrote, "A player is like a dove in your hand. If you hold that dove too lightly you could lose control and it might fly away. If you hold it too tightly, you could wound it or even worse, squeeze the life out of it. There is a balance in coaching."[85] Odle went on to describe an interesting encounter with a freshman player who disagreed with some instructions he had given on the court about the need to dribble lower or higher depending on the circumstances. Odle invited the doubting player, who believed there was only one way to dribble, into his office to talk about the issue. As they sat and discussed their different perspectives, Odle reached up to his bookshelf, brought down a book, opened it and read exactly what he had said on the court. The boy then agreed that "Coach" was probably right. Odle concluded the illustration by saying what the boy did not know was that he had written the book![86]

Odle's aggressively competitive nature made him focus strongly on winning games. Although he understood that it was much easier to win than to lose, he also was well aware that part of the coach's job was to help players deal with disappointment and pain. Therefore, he had to admonish his players to accept losses gracefully, "to take losing in stride" while "celebrating victory without gloating." Odle admitted that "he never learned what to say to players immediately after we lost." The best he could do was to counsel them "to keep their mouths shut" after a loss in order to prevent pouting or unwarranted demonstrations of temper.[87]

The Power of One

One of Odle's most important insights was that "coaching is teaching."[88] As his classrooms were student centered, so was the basketball court. Tim Diller, one of the many young men who played on Odle's teams, observed:

> Coach seeks out the driving, motivating forces in each of his players individually and uses these to help the individual improve personal and team skills. I feel that Coach considers normal physical skills secondary to mental conditioning and readiness.[89]

His classrooms were designed to enable students to develop their creative imaginations as well as their skills. He understood the teaching function of the coach in the same way. Not only did Odle view repetitious practice to be necessary to master certain fundamentals, but he also believed that basketball required creative imagination. The bottom line was that the coach's philosophy, theories and strategies were publicly judged in every game by the opposing team, by the fans and by the referees. One had to be good to withstand this kind of public evaluation.[90]

Odle has always believed that "playing on a varsity athletic team [especially at Taylor] is a privilege." Athletes have access to a unique platform when they enter the playing field or the basketball court to demonstrate their skills before an appreciative audience. The public performance places them in a unique position to exert influence over those who watch them play. Odle sought to teach his players that this privileged status carried with it great responsibility. If athletes were to be leaders it was necessary that they "prove themselves worthy of the trust and the leadership... vested in them."[91] Odle summed up his approach to his task as a coach when he wrote, "I believe that the real monument to coaching is what is left after the skills are gone. It is fine to turn out good ball players—but it is more admirable to turn out good men."[92]

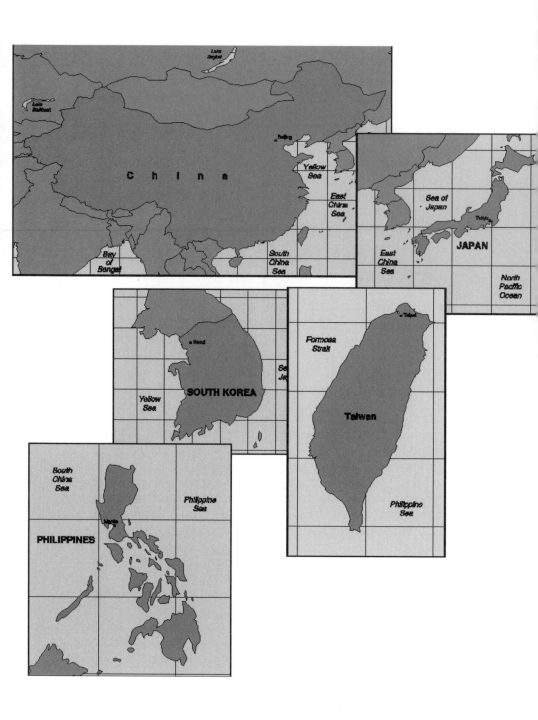

Chapter Two

FOLLOWING GOD'S ROUTE MARKERS

O ne day in February 1952 during the early morning hours the phone rang in Don and Bonnie Odle's Upland, Indiana home. "Coach" answered it and heard an operator's voice asking him to please hold for a call from Taiwan. The person on the other end of the line was Dick Hillis, co-founder of Formosa Gospel Crusades, later identified as Orient Crusades, Overseas Crusades, and finally OC International (OC). Odle listened as Hillis told him he had just come from a meeting with Madame Chiang Kai-shek, wife of the President of the Republic of China (Nationalist China). She was concerned about the morale of the Nationalist army defeated in 1949 by the Communist forces. Hillis and Madame Chiang had discussed the possibility of bringing an American college basketball team to Taiwan for the purpose of "moral and spiritual reconstruction." Would Odle be interested in such an opportunity for his Taylor Trojans? Because of his prior experience of success-fully taking his basketball team "on the road" in the United States, Odle was immediately interested in this new challenge and answered in the affirmative. This trans-Pacific telephone conversation set in motion the remarkable chain of events that greatly expanded the impact of the Taylor athletic program and led to the cre-ation of Venture for Victory, the first organization dedi-cated to evangelism through sports competition.

Venture for Victory's mission was clear from the moment of its creation in 1952. The new organization would sponsor a group of Christian college basketball stars on summer overseas tours, chiefly to East Asia. The primary objective would be to share the Christian Gospel with the audiences before whom they were play-ing. Don Odle's acceptance of this hitherto untried approach to missions qualifies him for the title "father of sports evangelism." At the same time it must be rec-ognized that many individuals, organizations and polit-ical realities contributed to the climate enabling VV to develop its unique ministry, first to the people of East Asia and eventually through its successor organization, Sports Ambassadors (SA), to the rest of the world.

Sign Post One: China – Ripe for the Gospel

Since its colonial days, the United States had impor-tant contacts with China notably in trade which greatly expanded during the early nineteenth century. The discovery of gold in California in 1849 led to a large migration of Chinese to the West Coast. Many were gold prospectors, others became laborers engaged in build-ing the Western railways. The Chinese were considered by many Americans as hostile aliens with strange customs and an indecipherable language. They were frequently viewed suspiciously as being clannish unable to fit in with American culture with its emphasis on individualism. This resulted in the passage of the 1882 Chinese Exclusion Act by Congress. Although many American movies portrayed Chinese in a sinister fashion, some such as D.W. Griffith's *"Broken Blossoms"* saw the Chinese as highly moral and ethical. In the 1930s, Pearl Buck, daughter of Presbyterian missionaries, published *The Good Earth*, portraying the Chinese as heroic hardworking agricultural people. Sun Yat-sen, regarded as the father of modern China, was considered by many Americans as a hero who advocated democracy and modernization for his country. China was seen as ripe for the Christian Gospel. Hence more American missionaries were led to China than any other area of the world.

East Asia, and particularly China, exerted a powerful pull on American Christians since Hudson Taylor's founding of the China Inland Mission. In the late nineteenth and early twentieth centuries, scores of Western missionaries poured into China resulting in the conversion of hundreds of thousands of Chinese. This missionary activity was met by both support and resistance. Many Chinese considered the missionaries as merely tools of Western imperialism, and like the Boxer rebellion leaders in 1900, reacted negatively to Christianity. Others such as Sun Yat-sen saw the positive contributions of missionaries, particularly in the development of schools and hospitals. Several Taylor University alumni answered "the call" to become missionaries in China in the period prior to World War II. Dr. Robert Ellsworth Brown was a student at Taylor during the first decade of the twentieth century and returned to teach chemistry and physics between 1910 and 1914. His wife, Carrie Mae Willis Brown, attended Taylor in 1907-8. Ten years later, the couple sailed for China, and Dr. Brown became Superintendent of Wuhu General Hospital in that Yangtze River valley city. The Browns were directly involved in the civil war in the 1930s. Floy Hurlbut, Gertrude Bridgewater Robson, J. Theron Illick, and Amy Spalding were other Taylor alumni who went to China. Charles P. Culver attended Taylor in the mid-1910s and went to China in 1920.

Missionaries serving in China had their lives changed dramatically by the tumultuous political and military events that unfolded in China in the 1930s and 1940s. On October 1, 1949 Mao Zedong proclaimed the People's Republic of China in Beijing, one of the most significant events of the twentieth century. Although nearly twenty-five years of civil war between the Nationalist forces led by Chiang Kai-shek (Jiang Jieshi) and the Communist forces came to an end, it resulted in the division of China. By December of that year, Chiang and his government had fled to the island of Taiwan and proclaimed the continuation of the Republic of China with American support.

Sign Post Two: Dick Hillis, China to Taiwan

One of the missionaries who had served in China and then became involved in Taiwan after 1949 was Dick Hillis, the man who made that early morning call to Odle in February 1952. Hillis was born in Victoria, British Columbia in 1913 of American parents. He graduated from the Bible Institute of Los Angeles (now known as Biola University), and joined the China Inland Mission (CIM) in 1933.

When Hillis arrived in China, he first spent six months in language school and then was stationed in Shenqiu (Shenkiu), a small town in rural Henan (Honan) Province located northwest of Nanjing. Because he was new to the culture and struggling with the Chinese language, Hillis was stationed with senior missionaries. However, shortly after his arrival, these missionaries were sent to another location leaving Hillis to struggle on his own isolated and lonely. When a telegram arrived announcing a ten day conference for defeated missionaries being held in Shansi, Hillis decided to go. It was there that he discovered one of the key principles he would incorporate into his mission—the need to provide opportunities for missionaries where they could be renewed spiritually and physically.[1] Hillis remained in Shenqiu from 1935 to 1941, traveling from one village to another as an evangelist.

During the time Hillis was studying at Biola, he became enamored of a student named Margaret Humphrey. Unfortunately Margaret did not share these emotions and dated Hillis' best friend. When he left for China, Hillis asked another friend to keep him informed every six months about Margaret. In the summer of 1936 Hillis received a letter telling him that Margaret was no longer dating his friend, but had been accepted by CIM and would sail for Shanghai in the fall. She arrived in October 1936 and was greeted by a letter from Hillis proposing marriage. He would wait six months for her answer, knowing that she would be occupied in language school. At the end of this period, she informed the director that she was being called to Shenqiu to become Hillis' wife. After their marriage in April 1938, the couple took up housekeeping in that town. Between 1938 and 1941, their first two children were born in China.[2]

The Hillis family suffered a number of crises as a result of the war between China and Japan. In January 1941 while Japanese armed forces were closing in on Shenqiu, Dick Hillis suffered a severe appendicitis attack. It was critical that he get to a mission hospital some 35 miles from home. He feared leaving his family, but he knew the friendlier Nationalist Chinese forces were in the area. No sooner had Hillis left than his family was informed by the commanding officer of the defending Chinese army that "the enemy is advancing and we have orders not to defend this city."[3] The next several days were anxious times for Margaret and the children. When Dick Hillis arrived at his destination, he discovered that the Japanese had already bombed the hospital and no one was able to help him. His only alternative was to return home and attempt the difficult journey to Shanghai. The family quickly packed essentials and began the journey by ricksha. The most dangerous part of the trip was crossing no-man's land between the Chinese and Japanese armies.

Several miraculous events occurred as they struggled to reach their destination. When they were accosted by a group of bandits who demanded their money, Hillis automatically handed the leader his name card on which was printed his Chinese name. Incredibly his Chinese surname was the same as that of the bandit leader who immediately exclaimed, "why your name is the same as mine... Kind sir we are brothers, we are members of the same family. We are now united."[4] The bandits returned all their money, gave them shelter for the night, and the next day guided them on their journey. When the family encountered hostile Japanese forces, they were confronted by an English-speaking general who had attended the University of Washington in 1936, the same time Margaret Hillis had been a student there. "The general greeted Margaret warmly. 'Tell me what you need. I shall fulfill any requests I can.'"[5] When Margaret asked for milk for her children and a place to rest, the general immediately ordered his men to provide for their needs. In the morning he gave them a pass which allowed them to continue on to Shanghai. Throughout this arduous journey, Hillis was suffering from excruciating pain which was finally relieved by successful surgery in Shanghai. The family was then evacuated to the United States.

During the remainder of World War II, the Hillis family resided in Texas and California. For one year Dick Hillis studied at Dallas Theological Seminary and then became professor of missions at Biola. Shortly after the War ended, CIM sent a number of male missionaries including Hillis back to China to survey the condition of their mission property and to ascertain the health of the Church. Hillis spent five months in

Henan province. After a CIM meeting in Shanghai, it was decided to allow the missionary families to return. In 1947 the Hillis family arrived back in Henan province and continued the work they had begun before the War. However, China was still not at peace as civil war broke out between the Nationalist and Communist forces.

World War II brought China and the United States together as allies. Chiang Kai-shek and particularly his wife Madame Chiang Kai-shek were widely regarded as devout Christians. Madame Chiang, the former Soong Meiling, had received a Methodist education in Georgia and had graduated from Wellesley College. In October 1930 Chiang was baptized a Christian in Shanghai, and "with his young wife beside him they repeated their marriage vows and pledged to follow a life dedicated to Christian principles"[6] Madame Chiang became an important voice for China in the United States during World War II. She was backed by the powerful China Lobby which included such luminaries as Henry Luce, *Time* magazine's publisher. Although there were critics of Chiang's Nationalist government such as General Joseph Stilwell who frequently commented on the corruption of his government, and American observer Edgar Snow who heroized Mao, by and large Americans were supportive of Chiang's Guomindang (Kuomintang) government. Following World War II, Americans watched with apprehension Communism's growing threat.

The town where the Hillis's were laboring was captured by the Communists who frequently harassed them. In 1948 Dick Hillis was arrested and interrogated. It was erroneously reported in the United States that the Hillis family had been massacred in their home. Later Nationalist forces regained the area providing a window of opportunity for Dick and Margaret Hillis and their five children to leave. While they were preparing to depart, a truck suddenly arrived bearing two missionaries from Kaifeng who had been sent to find out if they were still alive. Fortunately, the missionaries brought fuel which allowed the Hillis family to begin the dangerous journey by jeep to Kaifeng where they learned that CIM's director had ordered them to leave as quickly as possible for Shanghai. Heartbroken at being forced to leave his beloved mission field, Dick Hillis nevertheless accepted a position as teacher at the Bible Seminary in Shanghai where he remained until the Communists seized control of the city in the late summer of 1949. The missionaries were prisoners in their own compound with every movement observed and restricted until they were finally ordered to leave China from Tianjin (Tientsin) in 1950. Hillis and his family left China under difficult circumstances. Margaret Hillis was seven months pregnant at the time. The family, summoned to appear at the dock for inspection at 5:00 AM, was kept standing all day in the sun. Finally towards evening they were ordered to board a coal scow with some 200 other refugees. The

scow took them to an American ship anchored twelve miles off the coast. Finally, the ship docked in the United States on May 23, 1950 and Hillis settled the family in Yakima, Washington where Margaret gave birth to their sixth child.

Dick and Margaret Hillis and children in 1950

The difficulties like the ones the Hillis family experienced at the hands of the Communists convinced many Americans that Communism and Christianity simply could not co-exist. There was great fear of what appeared to be communism's worldwide expansion. At the end of World War II Stalin dominated most of eastern Europe. Then came Mao's victory in China which would be quickly followed by the outbreak of the Korean conflict in 1950 when North Korea attacked the South. There was increased Communist insurgency activities in the Philippines, and Ho Chi Minh stepped up his efforts to dislodge the French in Vietnam.

Don Odle expressed this widely held view about the threat of Communism, particularly in its opposition to Christianity:

> I do not pose as an authority on world conditions today or as an authority on the Far East, but I would like to express my opinion about Communism. It is anti-God and anti-Christian in every respect. It is impossible to be a Christian and at the same time be a Communist.[7]

With the collapse of Chiang's government to the Communists in 1949, Western missionaries departed from China, many moving to Taiwan. Chiang's determined statements that he intended to reunify China brought hope to many missionaries that they would eventually be able to return to their former mission responsibilities. Meanwhile they would continue to support Chiang and his government-in-exile. In Taiwan, Madame Chiang and others created a movement with considerable Christian influence focusing on the "moral and spiritual reconstruction" of Chinese society. Various missionaries realized that many Chinese living in Taiwan were interested in discovering additional ways in which the Church could widen its impact in that country.

Dick Hillis thought his missionary days were over in 1950, and he considered becoming a missions and church history professor at a Christian school in the United States. But in the meantime he decided to go to a Bible conference sponsored by a recently established organization known as Youth for Christ (YFC) to be held in Winona Lake, Indiana. There "Dick's war-damaged spirits were soothed in the peaceful atmosphere of the lakeside conference grounds. He basked in the fellowship of [old] friendships and made new friends as well."[8] At this conference he learned about what had been going on in the American evangelical community while he was serving in China. He learned about the work of Christian leaders including Billy Graham, Bob Pierce and Torrey Johnson, and he was introduced to the fledgling Youth for Christ organization.

Sign Post Three: Youth for Christ is Born

The world of the 1940s was shaped by the wartime experience. During this time of national crisis many American servicemen and servicewomen needed spiritual and recreational opportunities. Many were uncertain about the direction of their lives. Several young church leaders sensed that a new approach was needed to reach this young war time generation. Out of this concern emerged an organization known as Youth for Christ (YFC). A number of future evangelical leaders were part of YFC's inception, foremost being Torrey Johnson, Billy Graham, George Wilson, Bob Pierce and Ted Engstrom. It was this pioneer para-church group which proved to be significant in the early development of Venture for Victory.

Torrey Johnson was pastor of the Midwest Bible Church, a flourishing congregation in the Chicago area, and a professor of New Testament Greek at Northern Baptist Seminary. He was best known for his radio broadcasts, particularly a program called "Songs in the Night." Johnson was especially concerned about the servicemen who came to Chicago in droves on weekends looking for adventure. He wanted to find a way to reach these men with the Gospel. While in Minneapolis in April, 1944, Johnson attended a meeting organized by George M. Wilson, a local businessman. The meeting was held at the First Baptist Church and was billed as a "Youth for Christ Rally". Wilson was interested in combining the

Christian message with "clean excitement."[9] Johnson was so impressed by Wilson's idea that he went back to Chicago and immediately formed "Chicagoland's Youth for Christ", booking Orchestra Hall for twenty-one Saturday evenings. He chose Billy Graham, pastor of The Village Church in Western Springs, Illinois to be the preacher. The series ended with a rally in a 20,000 seat Chicago stadium. They then began a new series of rallies in Chicago, and at the same time they cooperated with George Wilson in Minneapolis and Jack Wyrtzen in New York in the sponsorship of many similar events in other cities.[10] During these meetings George Beverly Shea joined Graham and Johnson and the unique Graham preaching style was developed.[11]

The idea of creating a permanent Youth for Christ organization was born out of a meeting between Johnson and Graham on a fishing boat off the coast of Florida in December, 1944. A few months later Youth for Christ (YFC) International became an official organization when 42 delegates met at Winona Lake, Indiana. The purpose of the organization was to coordinate the Saturday night rallies "to capture and inspire American youth as no previous evangelistic movement had done." Johnson saw it as a "spearhead of return to a forthright Christianity—in America, Canada, the world."[12] The new organization adopted as its motto, "Geared to the times, Anchored to the Rock." Its evangelists including Graham wore "loud, hand painted ties and bright suits to communicate to America's youth that Christianity was not a dreary faith."[13]

Bob Pierce, a talented, energetic youth evangelist was an outstanding example of a young person attracted by the exuberance of the new organization. Eventually, Pierce founded World Vision Inc., a renowned humanitarian organization.

Robert Willard Pierce was born October 8, 1914 in Fort Dodge, Iowa. His parents were members of the Nazarene Church and Pierce went to Pasadena Nazarene College where he was elected student body president. While a student, Pierce met Lorraine

Johnson. Soon after their marriage they became involved in an evangelistic ministry focusing on youth. They spent some time working with Lorraine's father who was a minister at the Los Angeles Evangelistic Center, tried their hands at film making, and then returned to the field of youth evangelism.

While traveling in the northeast United States in 1945, Pierce heard about the recently organized Youth for Christ. He attended a YFC conference at Winona Lake, where he was contacted by a Christian businessman who wanted to sponsor a YFC rally in Seattle. The Pierces moved to Seattle and lived there for a little over a year before he was appointed to be Youth for Christ Vice President at Large. In 1947 he and David Morken, also affiliated with YFC, traveled in China for four months and held meetings in cities all over that country. On August 15, 1947 Pierce met Madame Chiang Kai-shek, and wrote to his family about the experience.

Bob Pierce

> We had the honor of a lifetime yesterday. Dave and I had the privilege of being entertained by Madame Chiang Kai-shek in her own home here last night. She gave us almost an hour... We told her briefly about Youth For Christ and she immediately showed interest, but Dave and I were a little disappointed at her lack of real spiritual insight. She rather thinks of Christianity in terms of Christian and social betterment... But she has had some real experience with God... I presented her with the Bible and she seemed genuinely moved.[14]

Pierce returned to China in May 1948 for another series of meetings and came face to face with the extraordinary hardships being endured by the Chinese. His daughter, Marilee Pierce Dunker, commented, "With each passing day he found himself more inextricably involved, unable to simply observe from a safe distance. My father went to China a young man in search of adventure. He came home a man with a mission."[15]

In March and April of 1950 Pierce along with Gil Dodds, an Olympic gold medalist, held a series of meetings in South Korea. The climax of this trip came in the city of Inchon where the record crowds numbered 15,000 for each of the last four nights.[16] Pierce returned home on June 1, and by the end of that month the North Koreans had attacked South Korea beginning the bloody Korean conflict.

Sign Post Four: Listening for the Spirit

Pierce's attention was clearly focused on East Asia and the serious crises facing that region when he came to Winona Lake in the summer of 1950. During one evening meeting held in the Billy Sunday Tabernacle on the conference grounds Pierce spoke:

Billy Sunday Tabernacle in Winona Lake, Indiana

> A cry for help has come to the Christians of America… Madame Chiang Kai-Shek… has asked for someone to come out to Taiwan and preach to the soldiers who have escaped from the Communists. Thousands have fled the mainland and have taken refuge on the island since the Communist invasion… They have left their homes and many of their family members behind. They are defeated and discouraged. Madame Chiang has already begun a women's prayer group in Taiwan. It is growing in size and fame. Now she wants desperately for the soldiers who have followed her husband to freedom in Taiwan to learn of the saving grace of Jesus Christ… Madame Chiang is pleading for someone to please come and preach the gospel to the thousands who need the message of hope…[17]

Through Pierce, Madame Chiang had extended an invitation for a team of missionaries to work on a short-term basis with the Chinese Nationalist troops. Pierce continued,

> There is a man here tonight who could go and do this very thing… This man has just returned from China and has himself experienced the pain of being ousted from the land he loves. Dick Hillis, I am going to ask you to come forward. Let us pray for you, that God would direct you into this new ministry if that is His will.[18]

Hillis reluctantly came forward and a group of young men including Billy Graham prayed that he would be led to Taiwan. But Hillis feared that Taiwan was doomed to fall to the Communist regime, and he did not want to place his family in renewed danger. Furthermore he was convinced his future lay in teaching in the United States. That night Hillis could not sleep. "He prayed and argued and wrestled with God."[19] He was overwhelmed by the realization that these Chinese soldiers had lost everything. He also understood that he was uniquely fitted to accept this challenge. He knew the Chinese culture and he could preach in Mandarin, something few North Americans had mastered. He also recalled meeting aboard ship bound for China immediately after the conclusion of World War II Presbyterian missionaries James and Lillian Dickson. The Dicksons had served in Taiwan from 1927 until 1940 when they were forced to leave due to the increasing hostility of the Japanese. The Dicksons and Hillis had talked extensively about their respective fields. As Hillis left the ship in Shanghai, Jim Dickson called after him, "If you ever have to leave mainland China come to Taiwan. The need is great."[20]

By the next morning Hillis realized he could not ignore this opportunity but he was torn by his need to care for his family who had gone through such trials and ordeals in China. He needed proof from God that Taiwan should be their field of service, so he asked God to confirm this call by certain signs. An important issue was how to provide support for Margaret and the children in his absence. He also requested God to provide a partner to go with him. One night as he was preparing to sleep, there was a knock on the door, and Hillis opened it to find a young man named Ellsworth Culver standing there. In his book *Steel In His Soul* Hillis recalled this incident.

> My name is Ells Culver... I heard the call for someone to go to Taiwan. The next day I heard that you were considering the idea but felt you shouldn't go alone.... I haven't been able to sleep since then... I think God wants me to go with you.[21]

Culver remembers that he had attended the OMS conference held two weeks before the YFC meeting at Winona Lake. Bob Pierce had been one of the main speakers at the earlier conference and had powerfully addressed the needs of Asia. Culver had been so deeply moved by Pierce's presentation that he later met with Pierce expressing his interest in going to Taiwan. In this conversation Pierce told Culver that he was convinced Dick Hillis was the man God wanted in Taiwan and that he should get in touch with Hillis.

COACH ODLE'S FULL COURT PRESS

Culver was a young pastor with a wife and a baby daughter. He was one of five children born to Charles P. and Nina Wilkinson Culver who had served as missionaries in China from 1920 to 1937. Charles P. Culver had been a student at Taylor University in 1915. Ellsworth (Ells), was their third son born in 1927. He graduated from Asbury College, and in 1949 went to teach at the American School on the Isle of Pines, Cuba. Returning to the United States he assumed the pastoral responsibility in a United Church of Christ congregation.[22]

Hillis explained that Culver would need to raise his own support and travel expenses. The plan was to conduct a three-month preaching tour in Taiwan and then return home. Would Culver be willing to accept these conditions? Culver went away to think about it and then returned one week later with an affirmative response. In a short time everything fell into place. Housing was provided for Margaret Hillis and the children, support was raised, and Uri Chandler, an OMS missionary, joined them.

On October 24, 1950, Hillis, Culver, and Chandler arrived in Taiwan to begin a three month preaching tour under the auspices of Youth for Christ.

Bottom left—Dick Hillis; Top left—Uri Chandler;
Top right—Ellsworth (Ells) Culver

There they were met by Jim Dickson and taken to the Dickson home which would be their headquarters. Soon after their arrival, they were summoned to a meeting with Madame Chiang. They were told "your ministry among the soldiers is of the highest priority... We will do everything possible to assist you."[23] An important way in which Madame Chiang helped their mission was to authorize the importation of thousands of copies of the Chinese translation of the Gospel of John. Madame Chiang's prayer group consisting of wives of many top Chinese officials provided transportation to the army barracks and arranged their preaching schedule with the soldiers. Every day the team was taken to a different base. The format was the same each time. They were transported on a weapons carrier and upon arrival were met by the commandant who served tea. Then they were taken to the parade grounds where "the soldiers were lined up waiting for the preaching to begin... Thousands of soldiers were commanded to be still and listen to the preaching of the word of God."[24] Hillis would preach, and then read a letter from Chiang Kai-shek affirming his own Christian faith and encouraging the soldiers to become Christians. Following this the Gospel of John was distributed to the troops which included a decision slip for the soldiers to fill out if they wished to become believers.

The missionary team was then confronted with the problem of teaching the new believers about the faith and integrating them into the churches in Taiwan. Hillis remembered that when he was in Shanghai the China Inland Mission had commissioned the translation of the Navigators Bible correspondence course. In November this correspondence course was ordered and two members of the Navigators were sent to help in administering the follow-up program. They corrected the correspondence lessons on the Dicksons' dining room table. On days off, Dickson took Hillis and Culver to many parts of Taiwan, introducing them to various people and their needs. As a result of these experiences, they developed a great burden for Taiwan, and a desire to evangelize the twelve million people who lived there. The island had only some 30,000 Christians and they lacked a vision to evangelize, according to Jim Dickson.[25]

As the three months came to an end, Dickson again challenged Hillis.

> Dick, you must come back. Taiwan needs you... I doubt that the Presbyterian mission board would accept you – your group is such a denominational mix. But perhaps you could begin a new mission. Think about it.[26]

Hillis and Culver did think about it, and on the way home, Hillis stopped in Washington, D.C. where he met with Dr. Clyde Taylor, the Executive Director of the non-denominational Evangelical Foreign Mission Association. The two men discussed the formation of a new mission which would be primarily involved in training the laity in order to strengthen the church. A new organization, Formosa Gospel Crusade, was co-founded by Hillis and Culver.[27] As their mission moved into other countries the name was changed to reflect this expansion; first to Orient Crusades, then to Overseas Crusades and finally to OC International. After the brief stop in Washington Hillis flew back to the West Coast and informed his wife and children that they were going to Taiwan.[28]

The Hillis and Culver families returned to Taiwan in the fall of 1951 and began a full time preaching ministry to the Nationalist soldiers. In January 1952 Hillis wrote to the mission headquarters then located in Los Angeles:

> We opened work under the new mission with only a handful of workers. We now have thirteen Chinese workers, twenty-seven aboriginal preachers in the hills, and eight American workers. Over 65,000 have made decisions of one kind or another. One and a half million gospels have been distributed. And 101,000 Bible studies have been sent out.[29]

Hillis and Culver traveled throughout Taiwan and were constantly looking for new ways to get the Gospel message out to the residents of that island nation. Culver remembers going to a basketball game in Taipei in which the Philippine Airlines Skymasters played the 1936 Chinese Olympic team. Culver's attention was soon diverted from the excitement of the contest to the enthusiasm of the fans. It was obvious that the crowd was enthralled by basketball. This experience triggered an idea. Perhaps if the mission could bring a basketball team from the United States and arrange for them to play top level teams in Taiwan, they would open a significant arena for evangelism. A few days later while Culver and Hillis were in Taipei they saw a crowd of eight thousand people waiting to get into a sports arena and Culver suggested his idea of bringing a Christian basketball team to Taiwan.[30] They agreed to work on bringing this idea to fruition. Do you think we could preach the Gospel if we had a Christian basketball team they asked each other?

> The first step was to get the backing of the first family. Dick made an appointment to discuss the idea with Madame Chiang. She responded with enthusiasm. 'If you can find the players we will sponsor the team and get them into the country'.[31]

Hillis and Culver immediately set about the task of locating such a basketball team. They began with the American organizations they knew best— Christian colleges and Youth For Christ (YFC). Culver recalls contacting one Christian college and inviting them to bring a team to Taiwan. However, the coach there responded negatively saying, "We are a university not a mission group, and besides, it has never been done before."[32] Other Christian colleges were contacted but these schools also failed to show interest in this opportunity.

COACH ODLE'S FULL COURT PRESS

Sign Post Five: Rejoicing in God's Faithfullness

At this point Ted Engstrom of the Youth for Christ organization entered the picture. Engstrom had become actively involved with YFC in the early 1950s, advancing to its presidency in 1957, a role he filled until 1963. Through his connections with YFC Engstrom learned of Hillis and Culver's search for an American Christian-oriented basketball team to come to Taiwan. He knew that Hillis and Culver had approached several Christian colleges, but these schools had failed to show interest in the opportunity. It was Engstrom who recommended Hillis contact Odle at Taylor University.

Engstrom and Odle had met during their student days at Taylor. They were both actively involved in athletics and played baseball together when Odle was a freshman and Engstrom a senior. Shortly after Engstrom's graduation in 1938, Dr. Robert Lee Stuart, Taylor's President, invited Engstrom to join his administrative staff and develop a public relations office. Engstrom accepted and upon his return to Taylor hired Don Odle as his secretary. Engstrom quipped, "Odle could type faster and make more mistakes in a single paragraph than anyone I knew!"[33]

Engstrom stayed at Taylor for two years and then took a job with Zondervan Publishing Company in Grand Rapids, Michigan where he remained until the early 1950s. At this time he became interested in the young YFC organization, and began working with them on a volunteer-basis. As a result of this work, Engstrom met many of the leaders of the organization including Dr. Robert (Bob) Cook, President of YFC from 1948 to 1957.[34]

Don and Bonnie Odle frequently attended the YFC summer conferences held at Winona Lake, Indiana where Engstrom introduced them to Billy Graham, Bob Pierce and Bob Cook. All of these men provided significant inspiration to the Odles. Engstrom was serving on the Taylor Board of Trustees and was well aware of the way in which Odle had developed the basketball

Portrait of Ted and Dorothy Engstrom located in the
Zondervan Library Galleria at Taylor University

team into conference champions. In addition he knew
about the trips to the east and west coasts combining
evangelism and basketball. Finally, Engstrom was rea-
sonably sure that Odle's willingness to try innovative
approaches to athletics would make him a good candidate for this venture into uncharted territory.

When the phone call from Taiwan came that
February morning in 1952, Odle most likely did not
review the intricate web of relationships and events
leading up to this extraordinary invitation. When he
hung up the phone, he probably did not fully compre-
hend the momentous adventure which lay before him.
A profound new idea in evangelism had been born!

Venture for Victory

<u>Chapter Three</u>

TRAVAILS AND TRIUMPHS: VENTURE FOR VICTORY'S FIRST TOUR

The Odles had never been outside of the continental United States before 1952, and admittedly had little real knowledge of the Asian culture. However, one of the foundational tenets of their faith was that "the hand of God moves in all our lives", and they believed that this unique approach to evangelism through athletics was divinely inspired. During their years as Taylor students, Don and Bonnie Odle had been involved in many prayer and Bible study groups such as those sponsored by The Holiness League. They had listened to many missionary speakers in church and in chapel including Taylor University alumnus John Wengatz (class of 1909), a pioneer Methodist missionary in Angola, whom Odle deeply respected, and E. Stanley Jones, Methodist missionary to India. They were personally acquainted with a number of Taylor alumni including Arthur Howard (class of 1934), athletic director at Taylor from 1936-1938, and later head of the physical education department at Lucknow Christian College, Lucknow, India. The Odles believed in worldwide evangelism and took the Great Commission seriously. They had agreed together that if the opportunity ever presented itself, they would answer the call to serve abroad. To the Odles, taking a basketball team to Taiwan was such an opportunity. This belief was a powerful motivating force which led Odle to seize this chance despite some daunting barriers.[1]

Birth Pangs

Revolutionary ideas are seldom actualized without heavy costs. There are usually difficult obstacles to be overcome requiring commitment, sacrifice and sheer tenacity. This was certainly the situation faced by Odle on that February day in 1952. Many questions raced through his mind as he contemplated the magnitude of the task which lay ahead. Would the Taylor University administration and faculty support such a daring venture? How would he find the right students to be a part of this experience? Would parents allow their sons to undertake such a mission given the potential risks of trans-oceanic flight and the political instability in East Asia? How much would it cost? How would he raise the necessary funds? How could he possibly consider adding such a monumental challenge to his already overfilled plate?

The quality of aggressive competitiveness and the tenacious, never-say-die attitude was needed if Venture for Victory was ever to become a reality. Odle first sought the approval of the University's five member administrative council. Following his presentation, the council members voted three to two to support the venture, a slim margin in the face of doubts and criticism.

Travails and Triumphs

While Odle would have liked one hundred percent support for the new initiative, he accepted the split vote believing in his own heart that "all the signals were go."[2] The door to an international evangelistic opportunity was opening and he was compelled to enter it.

By far the most daunting barrier Odle faced was raising the enormous sum of $10,000 in just three months. He did not have much experience as a professional fund-raiser, but he had developed a wide network of contacts in the surrounding churches and service clubs. He was in great demand as a speaker and was asked "almost every Sunday night to bring a girl's trio or a boy's quartet" to sing and speak at a young people's meeting or an evening church service.[3] This network of contacts was tapped in the effort to raise the money for the Venture for Victory trip. Odle and students would go to a church, tell their story and sing and speak about their faith and sense of God's call. They would place a collection box at the door asking the church members to support the trip if they felt led to do so.[4]

In addition to churches, Odle also approached civic groups such as Rotary. He remembers that he spoke over one hundred times in those ninety days. Most of the gifts were small—$10 or $25. Once he drove four hundred miles to speak in a church and came back with $18.[5] However, Odle believed that God was behind this effort, and that "the God who guides is the God who provides." He acted on this simple faith.

The largest gift received for this trip came from an unlikely source. At this time in Taylor's history, there was a small trailer house parked behind the gym and a retired missionary, Mary Thomas, had moved into it to be near her daughter who was the Dean of Women. One day, Thomas asked Odle to come and pray with her. During their visit, she told him that she was being led to give some money to the Venture for Victory trip. Much to Odle's amazement, this faithful, godly woman wrote him a check for $1000—a sizeable chunk of her own hard earned retirement money.[6]

COACH ODLE'S FULL COURT PRESS

Selecting the team members was a crucial step in preparing for the trip. Odle created a steering committee made up of Taylor University administrators, faculty, and students which included President Evan H. Bergwall; Rev. Maurice Beery, president of the Alumni Association; Professor Ralph Cummings, director of student personnel services and assistant professor of philosophy; Don Jacobsen, president of the junior class; John Nelson, vice president of the Varsity T-Club; and Coach Odle.[7] Odle applied three criteria to each student application. First, the applicant needed a positive testimony for Christ. A significant part of the Taylor ethos has always been to provide opportunities for students to share their personal Christian experiences both on and off the campus. Since Taylor was a compact academic community in an isolated environ, Odle knew the members of the student body very well, especially his athletes. His involvement with them provided him with the insights and information needed when making judgments about the applicants' Christian experiences.

The second criteria used in choosing team members was the ability to play basketball. Since it was impossible to take a full complement of players to Taiwan, it was necessary for each athlete to demonstrate unusual flexibility and stamina. Thirdly the applicant had to possess speaking and musical skills.

"Coach" fondly recalls the outstanding Christian athletes who participated in the first Venture for Victory experience. They were to a great extent responsible for launching the program on to its successful path. With one exception, the first team consisted entirely of Taylor athletes. This pattern of Taylor domination prevailed in the early 1950s but was gradually transformed with increased representation from other institutions. On the first team was Forrest Jackson, known

Forrest Jackson

66

as "Big Jack". He entered Taylor as a freshman in 1950. Each year he lettered in basketball and was named Hoosier College Conference (HCC) All-Conference all four years. In 1953 he set an Indiana season scoring record averaging over 27 points per game. He was Taylor's first All American in any sport and a charter member (1973) of Taylor's Athletic Hall of Fame. In a special Taylor University chapel service on September 22, 1995 honoring former VV players, Odle said Jackson was the first Indiana college basketball player to score 2000 points. Jackson was the only Taylor basketball player under Odle's coaching to be drafted by a NBA team, the Fort Wayne Pistons (now the Detroit Pistons). Jackson is a pastor in Dayton, Ohio.[8]

John Nelson

John Nelson lettered for four years in both basketball and football. He was best known in football as an outstanding receiver. He won All-Conference honors and was Indiana collegiate player's fourth leading scorer in 1951. Nelson was also an outstanding basketball star. He played a key role with Taylor's 1954 basketball team which proved to be one of the most successful winning seasons until that time in the University's history. In 1990 Nelson was inducted into Taylor's Athletic Hall of Fame. Nelson is a retired Chrysler employee living in Kokomo, Indiana.

Howard Habegger

Howard Habegger was raised in an influential Berne, Indiana business family with strong connections to Taylor University. He became a missionary in Colombia following graduation and in 1972 became missionary per-

Norm Holmskog

sonnel director of the Mennonite Church. He was also on staff at Hesston College, Hesston, Kansas.

Norm Holmskog was from Buffalo, New York and an athletic star in high school where he played basketball, baseball and football. Odle recalls that Holmskog's sister, a Taylor student, frequently talked about her brother's athletic achievements. Holmskog was given a full scholarship to a college in West Virginia. However, he did not like this school and transferred to Taylor in his second semester. After graduating from Taylor, he was hired as a basketball coach in schools in California and then Tabor College, Kansas. He received the Gates-Howard award in 1954. This award was established by two of Taylor's outstanding athletes, Joe Gates and Arthur Howard, and is given in recognition of outstanding athletic achievement.

Three of the original players—Don Granitz, Norm Cook and Bud Schaeffer—continued to be involved with Venture for Victory and have played significant roles in shaping its direction.

Don Granitz

Don Granitz had been a serviceman during World War II. Following his military discharge, he came to Taylor as a freshman in 1948. He grew up in the Christian and Missionary Alliance Church, and at the age of sixteen "received a call to the mission field."[9] He wanted to attend a college with a good intercollegiate athletic program and a strong emphasis on missions. He explored several evangelical colleges but opted to seriously investigate Taylor when his pastor recommended the school. Granitz

68

called Coach Odle and learned that a new football program was slated to be added to Taylor's athletic program that fall. Although he had successfully competed in baseball, basketball and track, football was his favorite sport. The prospect of playing at the intercollegiate level clinched his decision.[10]

At Taylor, Granitz showed outstanding accomplishments in baseball, basketball, football and track, and was the first in the University's history to win a letter in each sport. In fact he won twelve varsity letters. Odle called him "our greatest all-around athlete."[11] "Coach" noted that he could have also lettered in golf and tennis. In football, he was a quarterback, played both offense and defense, and was an outstanding passer and kicker. "Did you ever know a quarterback who led a team in tackles"?[12] He could throw a football 60 yards. "Coach" recounted that in one football game he "got off a quick kick for 85 yards!"[13] Granitz was voted most valuable football player for all four years, and made All-Conference and All State for three years. Following graduation from Taylor in 1952, Granitz became Taylor's football coach. His first year in this position was difficult since the team had lost several of its best players and they were defeated in all of their games.[14] However, the following year the team was greatly strengthened and ended the season with a record of three and three.[15] In the fall of 1954 Granitz was voted football Coach of the Year in the Hoosier College Conference. The Los Angeles Rams tried to recruit Granitz but he and his wife Jean were committed to missionary work. Subsequently they served for fifteen years in Brazil. Granitz was inducted into Taylor's Athletic Hall of Fame in 1973 as a charter member. In an article in *The Echo*, it was noted "his spiritual life and influence will never be forgotten... Granitz, Coach of the Year, was very instrumental in helping numerous athletes to find their 'Coach of Their Lives', Jesus Christ."[16]

Also on the first team was Norm Cook (class of 1951 — see page 94 for photo) whose roots were in

Warsaw, Indiana. Even though he had not previously played basketball, Cook was selected to be on the Taylor team coached by Gilbert Dodd. During the first game he scored the winning basket, and to Cook this was "a dream come true." Coach Odle noted that "Norm came to Taylor and scrubbed floors, washed dishes, and worked his heart out to stay in school." Cook also played football, but basketball was his favorite sport. Odle described him as "such a terrifically hard worker that he couldn't be kept on the bench."[17]

Since Odle intuitively recognized that it would be helpful to include at least one player from another Christian institution on the first Venture for Victory team, he invited Bud Stanley Schaeffer (see photos pages 104, 106), a recognized basketball star and graduate of Wheaton College, to join the squad. Odle knew well Schaeffer's remarkable skills on the basketball court because he had played against Taylor in Maytag Gymnasium when he was a Wheaton student. He dazzled the crowd with his "over the head dribble" even though the referee was not impressed and called a foul against him. Odle said many people called Schaeffer "unbelievable Bud." Norm Cook characterized Schaeffer as having skills "like a cat".[18]

Schaeffer asked how much money he would need to raise in order to make the trip, and Odle responded that each player would have to be responsible for a thousand dollars. Odle asked him to pray about it and a couple of days later Schaeffer wrote a letter in which he stated that he agreed to come and that this was a unique way to reach people for Christ. In this letter he stated, "I'll be glad to join this venture for victory."[19] Odle immediately seized on this last phrase, naming the team "Venture for Victory".[20]

"Coach" recalled that Schaeffer came to Taylor one week before departure time in order to meet the other team members and participate in the practice and preparation sessions. "Bud made a genuine contribution to the lives of the students. He spoke in Taylor's chapel, sang in the parlors, and offered a type of magnetic witness not often seen even among Christian young people."[21]

The months between the first public announcement of the VV project on February 10, 1952 and the team's departure for Asia in May were hectic ones. According to Odle, the tasks they faced "required all of their energies, talents, time and devotion."[22]

When Odle received the phone call in February there were many questions that went through his mind. There were many risks to the venture chief of which were the financial barrier, the question of Taylor University administration and faculty support, and the recruiting of a team. This was truly to be a leap of faith. However, as one progressed through the spring of 1952 these daunting barriers were surmounted one at a time. Financial support was assured, Taylor University was behind the effort, and the first team had been selected. With great enthusiasm Odle and the team prepared to launch this new evangelistic effort.

Bon Voyage!

The day of departure finally arrived. There was a sense of excitement in the air. One week before commencement the group gathered in front of McGee-Campbell-Wisconsin dormitory for one of the biggest "send offs" in Taylor history.[23] The doubts and criticisms of the early days had dissipated and now the faculty and students gathered to wish the team a heartfelt farewell. The media, including newspaper reporters and radio journalists, were there to cover the event.[24] Frank Anderson, a journalist for the *Indianapolis Times*, wrote: "The touring collegians don't expect to change the world for the better right away. But even if success against communism is measured in dribbles, basketball dribbles, they'll feel well rewarded."[25] It was indeed a momentous event in the history of Taylor. Odle and the team

The first VV team departs from Taylor University. Front row (left to right) —
Bud Schaeffer, Don Odle, Don Granitz; Second row — Norm Holmskog, John
Nelson, Howard Habegger, Forrest Jackson.

members were overwhelmed by the outpouring of love
and support from the campus community. There was
also apprehension mixed with the excitement and anticipation. Odle recalled thinking as he kissed Bonnie and
his son David good bye, "we may never return!"[26] At the
same time they all realized "as never before" that "God
was directing their lives." They had heard the call, seen
the vision, "and now they were prepared to embark on
the greatest adventure of their lives."[27]

The first leg of the trip was from Upland to San
Francisco. The team saved on transportation expenses
by driving manufacturer's cars to the coast. The group
traveled light. Odle noted that the athletes packed only
basketball equipment, Bibles, hymnbooks, and a message.[28] When they arrived in San Francisco, they conducted a series of meetings with young people further
developing their communication skills. The positive
reception they received in San Francisco encouraged
them and deepened their conviction that they were
doing the right thing.

Travails and Triumphs

Since there were no direct flights from the United States to Taiwan in 1952, several necessary stops were made along the way, the first of which was in Honolulu. A Honolulu newspaper reported that the team arrived "early Saturday and was greeted by some 500 natives at the Honolulu airport. The Taylor group received traditional leis upon its arrival at the field here."[29] That evening they played their first game against the Pearl Harbor Naval Base team and won 73-36. Forrest Jackson, John Nelson, and Don Odle were the high scorers. On Sunday, "team members conducted six evangelistic services on the island."[30] The team remained in Honolulu until Thursday, practicing twice a day in order to condition themselves for the tropical climate. They developed their ability to function as a team and prepared for the grueling schedule they would face in the next two and a half months.

March 2000 reunion of first VV team in Colorado Springs. Left to right—Norm Cook, John Nelson, Bill Lee (interpreter), Forrest Jackson, Don Granitz, Norm Holmskog

COACH ODLE'S FULL COURT PRESS

Epiphany In The Philippines

After the preparation time in Hawaii, the team members boarded the plane to continue their journey to East Asia. Their itinerary included short stops on Midway, Wake Island, and Guam, small dots of land "like postage stamps" in the vast Pacific.[31] They encountered some rather severe storms along the way. En route they crossed the International Dateline, still a momentous event in 1952. The players received small cards from the airline indicating they had been initiated into the "Celestial Order of the Vanishing Day."[32]

As the plane taxied to a halt on the tarmac in Manila, their first stop, Odle looked out the window and saw a large group of photographers and reporters. He remarked to his seatmate, "There must be someone important on this plane." The man replied, "Yes, I wonder who it is."[33] Odle was quite sure it had nothing to do with the team. In fact he was rather apprehensive as they approached the first Asian city. Stories of overcrowded conditions, assaults, robberies and civil war loomed large in his thoughts as he gazed from the plane's window. Uppermost in his mind was the fact that there would be no one in this city to meet them. They did not even have hotel accommodations, having failed to make any connections with missionaries before leaving Indiana. When the flight attendant came and told him he and his boys were to leave the plane together so the photographers could take their picture, Odle was completely mystified. The team was about to be confronted with concrete evidence of God's provision. It proved to be abundant!

Odle did not know that Ted Engstrom had continued to work on making a connection with the local Youth for Christ organization in Manila and had succeeded. One of YFC's supporters in the Philippines was John Sycip, a businessman whose company produced Soyalac, a chocolate drink. He in turn had contacted Regino R. Ylanan, secretary-treasurer of the Philippine Amateur Athletic Federation who was about to be named the general manager and adviser of the Philippine Olympic team headed to the 1952 games in Helsinki, Finland, and told him about this American basketball team coming to Manila. The Olympic team was looking for just such opportunities to play a team from another country as they prepared for the Helsinki games.

Odle agreed to play two games against the Olympic team in Manila's Rizal Coliseum. In exchange, the Philippine Olympic Committee paid all of their expenses in Manila and half of their air fare from Manila to Taipei, Taiwan.

The Manila Times for May 31 reported that:

> A seven man Taylor University basketball team headed by player-coach Don Odle blew into town yesterday afternoon for a brief stopover... Last night the Taylor U dribblers gave the small crowd present a preview by playing against the PAL Skymasters in a practice game. The crowd was very much impressed by their showing and it is expected that they will offer a stiff fight against the Philippine Olympic team tonight.[34]

The Americans played two games against the Philippine Olympic team before continuing on to Taiwan. On Saturday evening May 31, they went to Rizal Coliseum to face off against the Helsinki-bound Filipinos. The headline in one Manila newspaper the next day read, "Taylor Cagers Whip PI Olympic Five, 71-56." Two dramatic photos showing "Forrest Jackson tapping a rebound to Bud Schaeffer" and Schaeffer "leaping high for another attempt" accompanied the report. The article noted this was the first loss suffered by the Philippine team. It went on to report that the Taylor team "outshot, outran, and eventually outlasted" the Filipinos "despite the fact that they were limited to seven players."[35] The *Times,* called the team "Taylor U Crusading Cagers" and "Bible teaching dribblers." John Nelson and Forrest Jackson were singled out for special attention as they had "thrilled the... crowd with their spectacular long-distance push shots."[36] The press coverage and media attention, particularly in the Philippines, proved to be considerable during this and future summers.

The second game had a different outcome. This time the headline trumpeted "Olympians Triumph, 59-58." The game was played Monday, June 2 before 12,000 fans who jammed Rizal Coliseum. According to one newspaper, "the victory came after a fast, bruising 40 minute struggle that had the crowd roaring." After leading by one point at the half and by three points by the end of the third quarter, the VV team fell to their opponents who were described as "bearing down on its opponent with the fury of a wounded and angry bull." Coach Odle was quoted as saying that he hoped the team would be able to "come back on their return trip" because "you have fine basketball players here."[37] *The Times* focused on the fact that Carlos Loysaga, the star player on the Philippine Olympic team, was able to play in this second game and his presence made the difference. The following quotation demonstrates the kind of intense rivalry the Philippine teams felt toward this American college team.

> Carlos Loyzaga... proved to everyone that he is really the sparkplug of the Philippine Olympic quintet as he led his team to a 59-58 triumph over the Taylor University crusading cagers... It was a sweet revenge for Coach Fely Fajardo's charges who were humbled by the visiting American hoopsters with a 71-56 beating in their initial encounter.[38]

While the team was in Manila it also participated in evangelistic outreach activities including a large youth rally held on the basketball court of the Manila YMCA.[39]

As the plane left the runway in Manila heading for Taiwan, Odle reflected on the events of the past few days. It suddenly occurred to him that they had arrived in Manila "at the most opportune time in any four year period." Had they been a month earlier or a month later, "none of this would have taken place."[40] He also began to understand more fully that basketball was as important to Asians as it was to Hoosiers!

The experience in Manila was a powerful affirmation that this unorthodox concept—sports evangelism—was viable and full of promise.

歡迎!!
青年歸主籃球隊
WELCOME!
YOUTH FOR CHRIST CAGERS
PHILIPPINE AIR LINES

The VV team with Madame Chiang Kai-shek's "prayer ladies" and missionaries

His Strength Made Perfect in Weakness

In 1952, the team spent three and a half months in Taiwan, its main objective, in response to Madame Chiang's invitation. In *Venture for Victory*, Odle mirrored the belief in many American Christian circles that Chiang and his wife adhered to a strong belief in the Gospel. In part, Odle based his assessment on regular encounters with Madame Chiang Kai-shek and occasional meetings with the Generalissimo.

> Although we could not speak his [Chiang Kai-shek] language, the Madame interpreted for us. We could feel the love that was beating in that man's heart. He has a real love and compassion for his people, and he continues to fight Communism with great zeal. President Chiang

Coach Odle and Madame Chiang Kai-shek. The center characters state: "Work together with God". On the right—"To the Chinese Women's Prayer Group". On the left—"From the American basketball team Venture for Victory".

Travails and Triumphs

Kai-shek spends an hour in reading the Bible and in prayer every day before he goes to his office. I cannot doubt the sincerity of a man who spends this much time in prayer and Bible reading daily. I cannot doubt the sincerity of the Christian experience of a man who has compassion and love for his people as he does, a man who is interested in the souls and in getting the Gospel to his half million troops... We cannot judge the life of another, but I certainly was impressed at our meeting with President and Madame Chiang Kai-shek.[41]

In discussing the first meeting he and his Venture for Victory team had with Madame Chiang, Odle made the following observations:

The Madame spoke English beautifully; she spoke intelligently... She is a real leader and is inspiring to all her people. She made us feel very much at ease as we talked about Free China, the basketball team, and how the American boys liked the island of Taiwan. Then some of the deeper and more profound subjects were discussed. I shall never forget her first statement to me relative to their present position in Formosa. She said this: 'Right is always right, yet right is sometimes a risk.' We knew what she meant. They could have compromised with the Communists. By not compromising with them and doing what they thought was right, they were risking their lives, their country, and their future. But they did the right thing... She went on to explain the conditions under which they were living at the present time. She told me how much she appreciated the prayers of the Christian people in America.[42]

VV's main task was to play basketball against Chiang Kai-shek's army teams. Rather than playing under the name of Taylor University or Youth for Christ, the team chose to call itself "Kwei Ju", literally, "for Christ" or "return to the Lord." This phrase is also used in Chinese in identifying the Youth for Christ organization.[43] These Chinese characters were sewn onto their

79

uniforms, and the name "Kwei Ju" was used in the play by play commentary and in all the newspaper stories covering the team's games. Each time the Americans scored a goal, the spectators would yell "Kwei Ju".

By far, the most popular local team on the island was The Seven Tigers composed of high ranking officers in the Nationalist army who had played together for about ten years on the Mainland before being evacuated to Taiwan. During the first two VV trips Kwei Ju developed a unique relationship with The Seven Tigers.[44] Odle compared them to The Harlem

VV playing the Seven Tigers

Globetrotters and stated that fan loyalty was similar to that of Notre Dame alumni for their football team. "The Seven Tigers passed the ball with lightning speed and were very accurate shots in close."[45]

The first time the two teams met was in Taipei. Coach Odle was amazed when he discovered people had begun to line up on Friday for the game which would be played on Saturday. Dick Hillis told him that over 35,000 people had tried to obtain tickets for a stadium which only seated 8,000. On the night of the game, they discovered that the arena was seriously oversold and thousands of fans were milling around outside. This first game was very close. Odle remembered that the Tigers were leading by one point with three minutes to go when two of their players fouled out. The Kwei Ju team went on to win by twelve points.[46]

Approximately two weeks later, the two teams were scheduled to meet again in Kaohsiung. Once again, the stadium was oversold. A Taipei newspaper reported, "Nearly ten thousand fans packed a stadium for about half that number. It was impossible for the scheduled game to be played because every inch of the court was filled and a near riot ensued."[47]

Odle recalled the experience in detail in his 1954 book, *Venture for Victory*. The officials lost control and fled the stadium. Odle and his team were left to handle a crowd of ten thousand which was getting uglier by the minute. Even the Tigers had abandoned the effort. Odle was given access to the public address system and for about twenty minutes the team quieted the crowd by singing a song in Chinese and speaking. However, when it became obvious to the crowd that the game was not going to be continued, it became very unruly "throwing pineapples, bananas, rocks, and sticks onto the playing area." The situation became increasingly dangerous. Finally, Odle announced that the team would do an exhibition but they would have to get their basketballs from the truck parked outside. The crowd let them pass and they were able to walk out of the stadium unharmed. Once outside they discovered the truck with their equipment was gone so they just kept walking![48]

After this hair raising experience, Odle called the Basketball Federation officials and said they would have to be guaranteed security before they again would play The Seven Tigers. The next game was to be a week later, and the Federation promised they would guarantee safety. Kwei Ju arrived at the playing field and were met by soldiers with fixed bayonets and barbed wire entanglements. Every fan was required to walk into the stadium single file. Soldiers with machine guns roamed the outside of the stadium. Odle remarked, "I never saw such perfect control of a crowd though there was much tension."[49]

Kwei Ju was trailing the Tigers by twenty points in the fourth quarter. A time out was called, and Odle remembers "wishing it would last forever."

The heat, the concrete courts and the grueling schedule—two games a day for three weeks—had all taken their toll on the team and they were not playing their best. Odle rallied his exhausted players by reminding them that "it's no disgrace to lose a ball game, but when you've traveled ten thousand miles to do a job, you can't afford to do it halfway."[50] It was an "inspired team" that took the court. They were able to stop the Tigers, finally winning the contest by two points.

Hundreds of men came forward when they gave the invitation that night and one of the referees was among the first to respond. Later, Odle told the team members, "When you start converting referees, you're getting some place." Odle recalled, "After I got to my cot that night I tried to read my Bible, but I couldn't concentrate... What a wonderful feeling to go to bed at night tired for the sake of the gospel."[51]

Kwei Ju met the Seven Tigers twice more before they left Taiwan and won both games. Although their rivalry was intense, the teams respected each other's abilities and ended "the best of friends." They even conducted basketball clinics together. When the Taylor team left Taiwan, the Seven Tigers gave them a painting representing their team. The citation accompanying the painting read in part:

The Seven Tigers painting

> The American Youth for Christ basketball team came to Free China for evangelism and to fight Communism... They played our Seven Tigers five times. Their play, their friendship, and their fine techniques were appreciated. We were able to learn much from them.[52]

COACH ODLE'S FULL COURT PRESS

The painting currently is displayed in Taylor University's Helena Building near the President's office.

During the 1952 tour Kwei Ju played a total of 79 games in Taiwan and scored 5081 points. Ten thousand people "filled out decision slips" indicating their desire to accept Christ. Odle observed, "It was indeed wonderful to think that every time we scored a point, two souls came to Christ."[53]

The team returned to Manila in mid-August and played four games. Headlines and stories in *The Manila Times* for the week of August 12 tell the story of this last leg of the 1952 VV trip. They began the series by "crushing" the San Miguel Brewery team, 81-48.[54] Their second game was much closer as "the University of Santo Tomas dribblers battled furiously" against the VV team for "fully four quarters before losing by the close count of 69-67." Forrest Jackson's shooting was credited as making the difference for the VV cagers.[55] The August 14 *Manila Times* reported the "Taylor U Trojans" had "turned back" their opponent of the previous evening. "The Bible-preaching Taylor University Trojans last night posted their third straight victory of their second invasion of Manila by defeating the fast-playing Ateneo Blue Eagles, 78-71, in another closely contested game at the Rizal Coliseum." Forrest Jackson was "the shooting star" and the Americans "resorted to stratospheric plays" in order to bring the victory home.[56] The final game of the series was played against the M.I.C.A.A. (Manila Industrial Commercial Athletic Association) champion, PAL Skymasters. Despite their resolve to end the VV winning streak, the Skymasters went down to defeat partly as a result of Forrest Jackson's 29 points which brought his total for the series to 102. The *Manila Times* carried the following story:

> The popular Taylor University Trojans last night slaughtered the MICAA champion PAL Skymasters, 85-62 in their farewell appearance at the Rizal Coliseum. It was the fourth straight Victory for the "Youth For Christ"

Team in its second invasion of Manila...As if to leave something for local cage fans to remember, the towering Trojans uncovered their old mastery of every phase of the game with their deadly bullseye shooting and surprising the Filipino cagers with their lightning speed and real cage stamina.[57]

Using athletic competition as an evangelistic tool was more complex than it may have appeared to be at first. Even though the team sought always to present a faithful witness to the power and presence of Christ, the reality of human shortcomings was never far away. Odle remembered that during one game in 1952 he had an injured player and a sick one necessitating his own participation. As the game progressed, the referee called traveling twice against him while he was executing plays that he had used many times in the United States. The second time this happened, Odle in disgust threw the ball back over his shoulder unintentionally hitting the referee in the mouth. The force of the blow was great enough to ram the whistle against the man's teeth breaking one. The crowd hissed Odle strongly, and he removed himself from the game in a state of absolute dejection. He was so distraught by his own inconsistent action that he could not sleep. Sometime around midnight there was a knock at the door. When he opened it, he saw three military men standing there. He thought they were there to arrest him for breaking the referee's tooth. He woke his interpreter and discovered that one of the men had responded to the invitation that night and had shared the Gospel with his barracks mates. Now they wanted to know how to become Christians.[58] Once again, God had demonstrated that "His strength is made perfect in weakness."

When the players boarded the plane for home at the end of the summer they were all aware that they had had an unforgettable short term missionary experience, but none of them imagined that VV teams would continue to come to Asia in the years ahead.

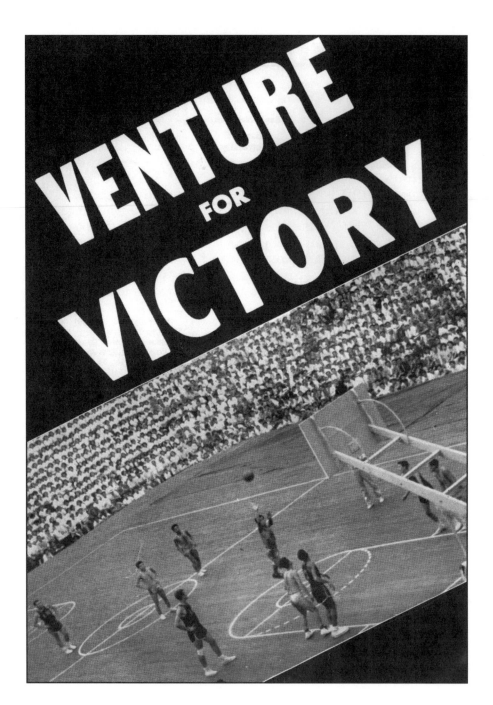

Chapter Four

THE POWER OF THE CHOSEN FEW

The 1952 team experience was a success but it became clear that Coach Odle could not effectively work on both sides of the Pacific. His energies would be required to organize future teams and seek financial support in the United States. Therefore, it was necessary to have contacts with missionaries in Asia, especially in Taiwan, who could facilitate setting up games and itineraries for future tours. The establishment of cooperative relationships between Odle and missionaries in East Asia, particularly those connected with Formosa Gospel Crusades, was crucial. In the early 1950s this mission was the one with the foresight to envision sports as an important evangelistic tool. However, individual missionaries from other boards also were enthused with this new idea.

Although some missionaries initially were hesitant

about following Hillis and Culver's lead in using sports as tools for evangelism, several were quick to recognize the opportunity for garnering increased visibility from the excitement and energy generated by the VV players. These missionaries were able to capitalize on this fact as they continued their work after the team's departure. A mutually supportive relationship had begun to develop between the local missionaries and the VV teams during the 1952 trip and this relationship continued throughout the fifties and sixties.

As one of the first short term missionary ventures, VV's primary objective was to help open new evangelistic opportunities with the ultimate goal of extending the Gospel message to larger and larger groups of people. Hillis, Culver and Odle all understood that if such an approach to missionary work was to succeed they would have to connect it strongly to the work of the career missionaries who would remain in Taiwan. Everyone recognized the importance of playing as many basketball games as possible. The short meetings conducted at half time provided significant opportunities to present the Gospel message to large numbers of people and the "decision meetings" held after the game led many people to indicate a strong interest in Christianity by signing up for the Bible Correspondence Course. However, it was also necessary to extend the team's efforts beyond the normal basketball court ministry thus maximizing the potential impact of these energetic young Americans. Hillis and Culver turned to Presbyterian missionaries James and Lillian Dickson to provide the link between the VV team members and the people who might not be able to attend a basketball game.

The Presbyterian Connection – James and Lillian Dickson

Lillian and her husband James had begun their missionary service in Taiwan in 1927 and were deeply

The Power of the Chosen Few

James and Lillian Dickson

involved in many aspects of Christian ministry. Dr. James Dickson founded Taiwan Theological College. He functioned as President of that institution and engaged in church planting and other types of evangelistic ministry. Lillian Dickson's ministry was multi-faceted. Her approach to missionary work was unique enough to demand a separate corporation, and she founded Mustard Seed in 1954, the umbrella organization which brought together her ministries to the poor, the orphans, and the sick and suffering people of Taipei and all of Taiwan. One of her evangelistic activities was conducting outdoor Sunday schools throughout Taipei. She founded An-Lok Babies Home for the children of lepers. Her organization developed a network of Mercy's Door Health Clinics, gradually spreading mobile clinics to the most remote mountain tribes. She developed a special ministry to young boys who were imprisoned for vagrancy, often sponsoring them so they could be released and returned to their parents.

One of the ministries to which Lillian Dickson had been called was serving the patients of a government run leprosarium. Her intervention made a dramatic difference in the lives of the patients. She was in the business of giving these otherwise hopeless, forgotten people for whom Christ died a reason to go on living. The government leprosarium had over 600 patients and its Chinese pastor had worked hard to convince Dickson that the lepers there needed her. She began her ministry to the leper colony by taking a fellow missionary and holding an evangelistic meeting.

Dickson was able to learn a great deal about leprosy and life in the colony. What she discovered appalled her. There was no doctor available to the patients. They had to cook for themselves, even those who had no hands. One day she learned that some of the leaders among the patients planned to hold a protest meeting about the lack of medicines, doctors, nurses, food, and clothes. Dickson knew that the lepers would not be able to achieve their goals by engaging in such a confrontation with the government, so she "faced the leaders and said, 'If you call off your meeting, I promise you that I will bring you all that you have asked.'"[1] Dickson kept her promise by first securing the help of another missionary doctor. The two women bought all the medicines they could afford and set out for the leprosarium. A clinic was organized and everyone who was able to do so came to the clinic for treatment. The doctor then went to visit the patients who were confined to bed.[2] Secondly, Dickson tackled the problem of providing a central kitchen so that patients would no longer be burdened with cooking their own food. She procured a space in the facility, provided a food storage locker, located former cooks among the patients, and supplemented the meager ration provided by the superintendent.

When Dickson first became involved with the leprosarium the suicide rate among the patients was very high, sometimes as many as three a day. One day she visited a patient she knew well who was confined to bed and asked him why he thought so many chose suicide. He answered, "Perhaps because they have nothing to occupy their minds... We have no touch with the outside world—no newspapers, no magazine, no radio, no educational movies." Dickson realized that her calling to be Christ's emissary in the world meant ministering to all levels of human need including that of intellectual stimulation and beauty. With this in mind she arranged for every room to be fitted with a loudspeaker so that the patients could receive radio broadcasts and hear beautiful music. She even convinced the United States Information Service to provide an educational movie every week.[3]

Dickson longed to be able to provide a suitable church for the Christian lepers. She wanted them to have "a place of beauty for their worship services and a place of dignity for funeral services." She began the project with a gift of $100 and built it as the money was provided. When the first VV team came to Taiwan in the summer of 1952, the church was under construction. It was not finished until October of that year.

The first VV team and every subsequent one during the 1950s and 1960s visited the leprosarium

Church for lepers

and played a game there for the entertainment of the patients. Odle recalls how frightening the prospect of this first visit was. He thought, "What if some of these flies would light on a leper and then on my sore knees or elbows? Wouldn't they transfer the disease?" When he handed a tract to a leper, he would jerk his hand back quickly so he would not make contact.[4] Norm Cook even arranged for them to play a leper team on one occasion. VV was behind for awhile, but they caught up. Cook recalled, "It was the only game in the history of VV that we never committed a foul! That guard would get his hands on the ball and head for the basket and nobody touched him. I mean he was clean all the way!"[5] Don Callan, a player on the 1955 VV team, recalled vividly how the challenge of playing a game in the leprosarium affected him. "I had never seen a leper before. They came up close to the court and I remember thinking I may be bumped out of bounds into the crowd going up for a lay-up. Boy, I tell you it scared the daylights out of us." His fears notwithstanding, Callan identified this experience as one of the most rewarding of the summer.

When the 1955 team came to Taiwan, they participated in the worship service at the Church of the Lepers and played a game at the leprosarium. They also found another new addition to the leper colony—an occupational therapy building. The new drugs were proving to be more effective in arresting the disease but even miracle drugs could not restore missing fingers and hands. Dickson believed what was needed was a place where they could develop new vocations and learn to live with their limitations. She wanted them to have enough confidence to become independent once the disease was under control. The team probably heard that this new facility had come into existence because of Dickson's perseverance in seeking help from another evangelical organization, The Christian Herald. On a trip to the United States in 1953 she had approached Dr. Daniel Poling. Although Poling was sympathetic to her request, he reluctantly told her that he did not have the money she needed. As Dickson got up to leave she said, "If you ever get any money designated for leprosy work, will you keep this in mind?" Dr. Poling assured her that he would but felt compelled to say his organization normally did not receive gifts designated for work in which it was not engaged. Only a few days later, Poling was amazed when he opened a letter containing a check for $18,000, the amount Dickson had asked for, designated for leprosy work.[6] Such simple and yet profound faith surely had a positive impact on the young VV teams who met Dickson.

One of the patients at the leprosarium was a man named Chhoa who had once been a skilled wood carver, but had lost his fingers to the disease. It had been twenty years since he had touched a chisel. But now he was encouraged to try. He strapped the chisel to one stump and the mallet to the other and was able to rough out the figure of a water buffalo, a gift for Dr. Poling. This was the start of a new career for Chhoa. He soon lost count of the number of carvings he made for presentation to visitors.[7] Coach Odle was the recipient of one of these carvings.

These visits to the leprosarium caused the team members to recognize more fully than ever that they could do nothing on their own, but if they were faithful to their vision and call, God would be there to bless their efforts. As the years passed, several of the VV team members became career missionaries. Witnessing first hand the power of faith in the life of a missionary such as Lillian Dickson must have been a great inspiration to these young men.

The Cook Connection

In the spring of 1952 Hillis and Culver were anticipating the arrival of Norm and Muriel Cook in Taiwan. Muriel Culver Cook was Ells Culver's sister, the daughter of Charles P. and Nina Wilkinson Culver.[8] The Culver family had deep missionary roots in China. Muriel was born in 1930 in Fuzhou, (Foochow) where her father managed a large Christian Herald orphanage, rescuing boys off the street and teaching them to make furniture.[9] Along with the happy memories of the colorful Chinese culture, Muriel also remembers the traumatic Christmas day when the Japanese bombed the city. One of her brothers was out riding his bicycle when he inadvertently encountered some Chinese soldiers who ordered him to halt. He turned his bike around and pedaled away as rapidly as he could as the soldiers fired on him. In 1937 Nina Culver became ill and needed surgery so she, Ells and Muriel sailed for the United States. Because of the war, Charles Culver closed down the orphanage and came home three months later. Muriel knew that "God had his hand on [her] life", and she had been called to go to China when she was just thirteen years old.[10]

Norm Cook, on the other hand, began his life far from Taiwan in Warsaw, Indiana. He was one of eleven children, largely raised by his mother. His growing up years were anything but tranquil. He describes himself as "a confused, bewildered teenager."[11] He belonged to a gang roving the Warsaw streets spoiling for a fight especially "looking for sissy Christian guys to beat up." Cook recalls that one night at about 11:00 when the town was closed up, he and two friends walked out on the pier in nearby Winona Lake thinking they would find somebody swimming. Instead, they encountered a Youth for Christ leader from Pittsburgh named David Nettleman sitting quietly on the pier. The young guys were using extremely foul language, and Nettleman confronted them with a question. "Would you use your mother's name in vain like you're using the Lord Jesus?" This got Cook's attention, and he answered the man, "No, because my mother loves me". Nettleman then said that Jesus loved them enough to die for them. At this point the other boys said, "Come on, Cookie, let's get out of here." They left but Cook stayed, and Nettleman subsequently led him to the Lord.[12]

Norm Cook

Cook graduated from high school in 1946 but had no plans for college. He had no contacts with a local church, but was invited to a Bible study in the home of Mildred and Roland Rice, OMS missionaries home on furlough from China. They opened their home every

The Power of the Chosen Few

Sunday afternoon to the young people of the community to come for a Bible study. At the end of the meeting Mildred Rice, who was leading the Bible study, asked the group to stand, hold hands in a circle and each say a short prayer. This made Cook extremely nervous. "I am not a hand holder!" Furthermore, he had never prayed out loud, but it was this experience that "unlocked something inside of him."[13] It was at the Rice Bible study that Cook first encountered Muriel Culver. At this time Charles Culver was a deputational secretary for OMS, and the family cared for furloughed missionaries in their large Winona Lake home.

Shortly after meeting, Norm and Muriel began dating. On one of these occasions they went to see a Taylor University basketball team play against Manchester College in North Manchester, Indiana. Taylor's team was "pathetic", and on the way home he said to Muriel, "This is not right. Christians should be the best. I could play better ball than that. Do you think if I went to Taylor I could play basketball and help the team?" Since Muriel was "quite smitten by Norman" and wanted him to go to college she replied, "Why don't you apply and see?" He followed her advice, applied and was accepted.[14]

In January, 1947, Norm packed a duffle bag and a suitcase and headed to Taylor with $50 in his pocket. When he arrived on campus he was taken to McGee-Campbell-Wisconsin Dormitory. "It was the finest building I'd ever seen", recalled Cook. He was taken to a fourth floor room which was cold, dusty and totally empty save for beds with a bare mattress and pillows. In Cook's eyes the room was luxurious. There was an inside bathroom, and his own bed, both of which he had never before experienced.[15] Cook majored in history with minors in Greek and English. Until his junior year he was planning to become a coach. But while he was researching a paper on U.S and China relations from 1937 to 1947 for Professor Grace Olson's history course, Cook began to rethink his future goals. "The idea of China began to grow in my heart—I knew I'd be a missionary." In his third year at Taylor, Cook took a long walk one day, knelt in the grass and asked, "Lord, what would you have me to do?" In the fall of 1949 Cook gave a testimony in a Youth Conference meeting held in Maytag Gymnasium in which he said, "God has called me to China and I am going to go there or die trying." Muriel was in the audience. She recalled that even though she and Norm had kept up a regular correspondence—Norm wrote her every day—and their relationship was growing, "they were very careful not to declare their love." Although she knew she was in love with Norm, she was waiting for him to determine what he was going to do with his life.[16]

Muriel Culver came to Taylor as a student when Norm was in his junior year and they married in June 1950. Norm graduated in January 1951 and the couple moved to Marion, Indiana where he was employed as the pastor of the Home Park Methodist Church.

Co-author Jessica Rousselow-Winquist with Ells Culver and Muriel Cook—Summer 2001

During two summers he also attended the Winona Lake School of Theology that was connected to Fuller Seminary.

It was at Winona Lake that the Cooks heard Hillis speak about the needs in Taiwan. Hillis and Muriel's brother, Ells, had been to Taiwan and had come back to recruit missionaries. Muriel and Norm Cook felt led to answer "the call." Hillis told the young couple that he would be gone for about two weeks but during that time they were to do three things: consult with people who knew them well; consult the Scriptures; and pray for confirmation of the call. "The Lord gradually confirmed in our hearts what we should do", recalled Cook.[17]

The Power of the Chosen Few

The Cooks raised their support in four months and in the spring of 1952 they were making their way across the United States, speaking in churches about the needs in Taiwan. While they were in Indianola, Iowa, Norm Cook received a call from Don Odle telling him that he had been contacted by Hillis who had requested a basketball team to come to Taiwan and play a series of games during the upcoming summer. Odle wanted Cook to join the team and to work on organizing the schedule ahead of the team's arrival. Without hesitancy Cook answered affirmatively, saying "There are some things you don't need to pray about."[18]

When the Cooks arrived in Taiwan, Hillis was still working under the auspices of YFC and held the title Vice President of Asia YFC. However, the Hillis's, Culvers and Cooks immediately committed themselves to the task of creating a mission with a unique approach to reaching the people of Taiwan. As the organizational structure of the new mission, Formosa Gospel Crusade, emerged Hillis assumed the directorship and Cook was appointed to be Field Director in Taiwan, a position which he held until 1968. The Cooks characterized Hillis as "a servant leader who always set the example trusting his young workers with large responsibilities. Muriel Cook stated, "We loved him and killed ourselves for him. He believed in us and always treated us honestly and fairly."[21]

Cook set to work immediately upon their arrival, lining up two to three games a day for the VV team which was scheduled to arrive in June. In fact, he scheduled 87 games in 40 days. Cook stated, "these guys were strong and healthy. They were not there to sightsee. They were there to lead people to Jesus."[19] Cook made sure the team had abundant opportunities to fulfill this mission. In addition to setting up the grueling schedule of games, Cook played on the team. This first VV experience set the pattern for the next twenty-four years. He continued to play on the teams for about ten years and when it became necessary, he coached the squad in Odle's absence.

Cook was indispensable to VV's success. He set up numerous itineraries for the VV teams when they visited Taiwan. During the year Cook met with the Basketball Federation in Taiwan and worked out the details of the schedule. He went to factories, schools, U.S. military bases and worked with missionaries in planning games. Cook observed, "I'd go to the U.S. Embassy. My connection to VV gave me entry and I really used it." He also added, "This was the way I got to Madame Chiang."[20] The itineraries were always packed. Cook used contacts with other missionaries such as Lillian Dickson to arrange visits to refugee camps, prisons, the leprosarium, schools, churches and outdoor Sunday schools. In all these venues the team members engaged in a variety of evangelistic activities. He arranged for the team to play in small and large stadiums, and sometimes there was no stadium at all, only an outdoor court. Odle described several of these experiences in his book about the 1952 and 1953 trips. On one occasion, the outdoor court was located on the side of a hill and during the first half of the game VV had to dribble uphill,

Norm Cook and VV team with a Taiwan squad

and downhill during the second half allowing them to have "one of the best fast breaks" they had had all summer. On another occasion they played a game in the mountains during a driving rain storm on a dirt court turned to slippery mud.[22] Cook saw to it that the teams did not just stay in Taipei. Every summer they traveled to other cities in Taiwan as well as visiting the more remote villages on the Island. Odle described one such trip deep into the mountains where they visited the Tyal people. In order to get there they first borrowed a jeep from one of the missionaries and drove as far as they could. Then they started walking. They visited several villages and were given a friendly reception in the churches that had been planted by James and Lillian Dickson.[24]

As a result of these experiences, Norm Cook learned to be very resourceful. He became extremely knowledgeable not only about Taiwan but also other parts of East Asia. "No graduate from Taylor ever knew the Orient as well as Norm Cook," declared Odle.[23] Cook became a missionary statesman, impacting the whole island of Taiwan with the Gospel.

Muriel Cook also developed her own sphere of ministry. Along with a Chinese woman co-worker, she began street evangelism. She visited every home within walking distance sharing the Gospel and developing friendships with the women who ran the shops. After realizing that these women were interested in visiting an American home, she developed Sunday afternoon open houses serving an English style "high tea." Eventually she found herself teaching seven Bible classes a week in English. "Everyone wanted to learn English, and I said I would teach them if I could use the Bible. I had classes with some important people such as newspaper reporters and photographers for the *China Daily News* and top officers in the Chinese military. Madame Chiang came once to be a speaker."[25]

Cook noted that some missionaries at first did not see the value of sports. There were times when there was tension within the mission and frequently this was the main subject at pastor's conferences. Cook reflected that for nine months out of the year missionaries were restricted in their work, but when the VV team came on the scene numerous opportunities opened to them. Cook also is convinced that "we [the VV teams] raised the standard of Asian basketball."[26]

There is no question but that the Cooks exerted a powerful impact on the young men who came to Taiwan to play basketball. For example, Roger Jenkinson, a former VV player summed up Cook's missionary zeal and dedication as follows: "Norm Cook will go down in my estimation as one of the great missionaries in that area [East Asia] of the world. He learned Chinese, and went to places where no other missionary would go."[27]

In 1968 Cook was asked to return to Overseas Crusades headquarters in California and assume the position of Executive Director of Personnel, and Asia Area Director. He did so on the condition that he would be able to go out to the field at least once a year. In 1981 Cook left Overseas Crusades to become a professor at Multnomah Bible College.

Expanding to the Philippines

By the end of 1952 it became apparent that the needs in East Asia extended far beyond Taiwan. The VV team had stopped in the Philippines at the beginning and end of their summer tour and had found the Filipinos as receptive to basketball as the Chinese were. Therefore, it was decided to expand the ministry of Formosa Gospel Crusades. Accordingly the name was changed to Orient Crusades and new missionaries were recruited. One of the first Orient Crusades missionary couples to go to the Philippines was Charles (Chuck) and Elisabeth (Betty) Holsinger. They chose Orient Crusades largely because of its commitment to sports evangelism.

Chuck Holsinger was born in Red Bluff, California in 1924.[28] His father was a minister. In the fall of 1942, Chuck entered Wheaton College as a freshman, but that December his college education was interrupted when he was called to active duty in the army. Holsinger's unit set sail from San Francisco in July 1943, and eventually arrived in Guadalcanal where he was assigned to the 25th Infantry Division. In September his unit

Holsingers

invaded the island of Vella LaVella. Here he observed first-hand the work of Christian missionaries who had a lasting influence on his life. On January 11, 1945, Holsinger took part with the 25th Division in the landing on the island of Luzon in the Philippines. "In a matter of hours Filipinos with tattered clothes, half-starved bodies, haggard and drawn faces began to emerge from hiding. The joy of liberation had begun."[29] For his bravery in battle, Holsinger was awarded a silver star in June 1945.[30]

After the war, Holsinger returned to Wheaton where he met and married Elisabeth (Betty) Hermansen, a classmate. Holsinger graduated in 1949 with majors in history and Bible and immediately began coaching football at his alma mater and working with church-related youth ministries. He also received a master's degree at Wheaton in New Testament Biblical Literature in 1952.

Holsinger's war experiences in the Pacific theatre had caused him to consider mission service in East Asia. On Easter Sunday 1953 he was challenged to go to the Philippines as an athletic missionary to work with Filipino youth. In the early fall the Holsingers arrived in Manila where Chuck was appointed Orient Crusades field director. He traveled throughout the Philippines teaching basketball and preaching to young people.[31]

His main work was evangelism and he traveled "up and down the islands" conducting coaching clinics and preaching the Gospel. In 1953 he also coached a Chinese Team in the Asian Games. Two of the players on this team were converted and became coaches of Nationalist Chinese teams. Holsinger asked Wheaton College to invite the Republic of China team to the United States. The netters came and barnstormed the Christian college circuit, playing against Taylor, Wheaton and Biola. This visit of a Chinese team to these colleges contributed to the growing interest in continuing to send American teams to Asia.

Although no VV squad came to Asia in 1954, Orient Crusades did send a male quartet to the Philippines. Holsinger set up the program for them to conduct meetings. As the quartet traveled through the country, they were repeatedly asked, "Why aren't you guys playing basketball?" In response to this over-whelming interest in the sport, the young men some-times played informal games with local teams. The reception given the quartet served to demonstrate that the Filipinos were very interested in having VV return to their country and planning was begun for the third trip. Unfortunately, Holsinger was ill with hepatitis in the summer of 1955 and was unable to help VV in a significant way that year.[32]

In December 1955 Holsinger left the Philippines and went to Taiwan where he became the athletic director and coach at Morrison Academy, a school for sons and daughters of missionaries. In this posi-tion he worked as advisor/coach with the Chinese Basketball Federation laying the foundation for the next American teams. Holsinger worked with Cook dividing the responsibility for scheduling VV games in Taiwan. In addition, he used his own teams in sports ministry when they played other schools in Taiwan. Holsinger remained at Morrison Academy until 1974 when he returned to the United States and took up various positions with Overseas Crusades including Executive Vice President (1982-1998), and Assistant Area Director for Asia and Latin America. Holsinger returned to Asia as a Sports Ambassadors/Venture for Victory team director in 1975 and 1976.[33] In 1992 Wheaton College honored the Holsingers by granting them the "Alumni of the Year Award."[34]

"Short Term" to Career Missionary

One of the long term results of the Venture for Victory experience was that several players were challenged to enter full time missionary work. Bud Schaeffer, a member of the 1952 VV team, was one such player. He and his wife Alice chose to go under the auspices of Orient Crusades for the same reason as the Holsingers, that being the mission's involvement in sports evangelism.

Schaeffer was born in 1927 in Franklin, Pennsylvania. He was influenced by his mother's Christian faith, but she died when he was 14 years of age. He then moved to Michigan City, Indiana where he lived with his sister and brother-in-law. He was an athlete in high school, graduating in 1945. He enlisted in the Navy, and was stationed at the Great Lakes Naval Base. He traveled with the Great Lakes Navy basketball team (they played against the Big Ten teams) until his discharge in 1946 at which point he entered Wheaton College where he majored in biblical studies. While at Wheaton, Schaeffer played baseball and basketball; in the latter sport he was an all-conference guard for four years. As a Wheaton student he sang on many gospel teams and worked during the summers at Winona Lake.

Both the Minneapolis Lakers and the Philadelphia Warriors recruited Schaeffer to play for them, but he had strong convictions against playing on Sundays, and so did not accept their offers. For one year Schaeffer played professional basketball with the Boston Whirlwinds. This team played exhibition games against the Harlem Globetrotters in forty-four states and Cuba. Later, he played with the U.S. All Stars in Latin America, another team that competed against the Harlem Globetrotters in exhibition games. In 1951 he enrolled in Fuller Theological Seminary, and married Alice Marie Brown, a gifted artist and soprano soloist.

In the spring of 1953, as Odle was preparing for the second VV trip, he realized he needed Bonnie's support. She was reluctant to be the only woman on the trip and expressed her desire for Alice Schaeffer to come along. Odle telephoned Schaeffer inviting him to join the summer VV team requesting that Alice join Bonnie on this trip. Schaeffer would have to raise his own support but "Coach" would find the financial resources to support the two wives. The Schaeffers had just learned that Alice was pregnant, but she agreed to go and not reveal this fact until the summer was over.[35]

Schaeffer's experience with the first two Venture for Victory teams created in him a strong interest and deep concern for the Filipino people. In May 1955 the

Schaeffer with the 1960 VV team

The Power of the Chosen Few

Schaeffers left for the Philippines as missionaries with Orient Crusades. Three of the four Schaeffer children were born in that country. For twelve years they lived in the Philippines, where Bud directed, coordinated and often played on Venture for Victory basketball teams. During the rest of the year Schaeffer worked in youth camps, conducted sports clinics, and organized pastors and youth conferences. His basketball clinics enabled him to gain entry into schools in the Philippines. Another way in which Schaeffer used sports to evangelize was through "crusader teams". These squads were made up of career missionaries who traveled throughout East Asia playing games in a variety of venues much as VV did in the summers. The missionary teams doubtless contributed to keeping interest high for VV. Schaeffer planned itineraries for the VV teams along with Tine Hardeman, a Westmont College graduate who had played on the third VV squad in 1955. Like Holsinger and Schaeffer, Hardeman chose Orient Crusades because it afforded the opportunity to use sports as a means of ministering. He became the coach at Faith Academy in Manila, a school for missionary children. This assignment made it possible for him to continue to play along with Schaeffer on VV teams throughout the fifties and sixties.

In 1956 Schaeffer coached the Nationalist Chinese Olympic team. He also had a leading role in the film *Venture for Victory* produced in 1962 by Ken Anderson Studios of Warsaw, Indiana (see photo on page 170). For three years in the mid 1970s the Schaeffers lived and served in Australia. In 1967, Orient Crusades, which had now been renamed Overseas Crusades, asked Schaeffer to return to the United States as head of a new division of its organization known as Sports Ambassadors, a continuation of VV. Under Schaeffer's leadership the program was expanded to include both basketball and baseball teams not only to East Asia and South America, but also to Europe and Australia. In addition, an innovative program of women's basketball teams was launched. Robin

Cook, Schaeffer's son-in-law, is currently director of Sports Ambassadors.

The symbiotic relationship which developed between career missionaries and VV brought great benefits to all who were involved. Certainly not all missionaries saw the value in this new approach to evangelism resulting in some tension. However, when VV came to Taiwan they opened numerous opportunities for missionaries to take advantage of during the rest of the year. Concurrently, Odle and the young men who came to East Asia were confronted with the reality of the missionary experience. It was one thing to listen to furloughed missionaries speak in their home

Schaeffer preaching the Gospel at half time

churches. It was quite a different experience to come face to face with the suffering of orphans, the despair of refugees, and the isolation and hopelessness of lepers. VV players who chose to return to East Asia as career missionaries did so with their eyes wide open to both the needs of the people and the redemptive potential of the Gospel.

The Power of the Chosen Few

Chapter Five

CRUSADING CAGERS: 1953-1957

During the mid 1950s VV continued to make additional contacts with the help of missionaries, and political and military figures resulting in expanded travel opportunities and the chance to play against new teams. Gradually, VV's reputation increased both overseas and in the United States. Another change during the middle part of this decade was Odle's decision to select players from a wider group of Christian colleges than previously. The team's phenomenal winning streak continued. VV played games in a wide variety of venues concentrating primarily on contests with local teams. However, in the Philippines, teams from the professional M.I.C.A.A. League sought the opportunity to compete against the "Bible preaching Cagers," an expression frequently used in the Philippine press to describe VV. Regardless of the situations in which they competed, its members never lost sight of their primary evangelical mission. At the same time, it must be acknowledged that the reputation of VV as a winning basketball team was greatly enhanced by the considerable press coverage given them especially in the Philippines.

Solidifying Relational Ties -1953.

The second Venture for Victory trip occurred in the summer of 1953. The team's itinerary included a stop over in Hawaii where the squad practiced, returning to the Philippines and Taiwan and for the first time visiting Japan and Korea. Unlike the first team which was almost entirely made up of Taylor University players, this squad included four men from other colleges. Floyd Habick represented Northwestern College, Minneapolis; Paul Hoffman, Manchester College; Jerry Carey, Anderson College; and Buddy Peyton, Asbury College. Howard Habegger and Forrest Jackson, veterans of the 1952 team, were joined by Don Jacobsen as representatives from Taylor. Bud Schaeffer came from Fuller Seminary. Norm Cook and Coach Odle completed the squad.

Don Jacobsen chose to forego participating in graduation ceremonies in order to join the other members of VV in California. Odle needed a musician and a business manager, two roles Jacobsen was able to fill. He kept meticulous financial and narrative records of the summer's experience.[1]

Jacobsen grew up in Hastings-on-Hudson, New York and was active in sports including basketball during his high school

Don Jacobsen

Crusading Cagers: 1953-1957

Don and Shirley Jacobsen (third and fourth from left) with John and Jane
Nelson (first and second from left), Alice and Bud Schaeffer, and Jean and Don
Granitz at reunion in Colorado Springs, March 2000.

years. Because of his tennis skills Odle became interested in having Jacobsen attend Taylor. Even though
Jacobsen had known only one Taylor student, he
decided to apply. During the summer of 1949 Odle
helped to expedite the processing of his application.
Jacobsen recalls that he left Pennsylvania Railway
Station in New York City bound for Upland, a nineteen
hour trip. Jacobsen was a member of Taylor's tennis
team for four years, and he played football when he
was a junior and senior. He nearly left Taylor in the
spring of 1950. However, due largely to Odle's intervention, Jacobsen chose to continue his studies in business at Taylor. During the summers Jacobsen worked
at Camp of the Woods where he met Shirley Lunde,
originally from New Haven, Connecticut. Shirley had
a brother who attended Taylor, and she transferred
there in her junior year graduating with the class of
1952. Don Jacobsen and Shirley Lunde were married
in 1954 and had two children, both of whom graduated from Taylor as did their spouses.[2]

The year 1953 was the first time women were a
part of the VV tour. The dynamics of the group were
changed by the presence of Bonnie Odle and Alice
Schaeffer, both of whom had been their husband's

Schaeffers and Odles arriving in East Asia

chief supporters from the beginning. The Odles and the Schaeffers understood how vital it was for the two wives to experience the program personally. Bonnie characterized her role as "supporter" and Don said she was "the mother to the guys on the team".[3] In 1953, it was not always easy to be thousands of miles away from one's home and family. Obviously one could not communicate via e-mail, and even telephone conversations were sometimes difficult. The Odles had left their seven year old son, David, with his grandparents for the summer. Although they knew he would be well cared for, they still experienced the loneliness and pain of the long separation.

Besides acting as "mother figures" and chief confidantes to the young men, the two women helped with the mundane day to day needs of the group. During the team's stay in the Philippines Bonnie and Alice remained in Manila while the team traveled south. The two women conducted a series of meetings in which they used their own considerable musical, artistic and communicative talents to share the Gospel. In Bonnie Odle's words, "The experience enlarged our lives."[4]

The team spent the first month in the Philippines.

Crusading Cagers: 1953-1957

When their plane landed in Manila, a large group of Christians met them and according to Jacobsen they were "ushered through customs like a bunch of dignitaries... Pictures were taken and people stared at us as though we were actually great."[5] The following day they went to the courthouse where they were introduced to Arsenio Lacson, Manila's mayor. He was scheduled to toss the first ball that evening to signal the opening of a six game series.[6] The visit with the mayor was followed by lunch with reporters at the Bay View Hotel.[7] Later that week they met Major General Calixto Duque, the Army Chief of Staff of the Philippines, and visited Jorge Vargas, President of the Philippine Athletic Association.[8]

The team meets Major General Calixto Duque

In addition to playing their scheduled games, the team members conducted meetings and held basketball clinics in a variety of venues. In the process they encountered many different dimensions of Philippine culture. They experienced great economic disparity when they held a service in the "poorest section" of Manila. Jacobsen wrote, "Never in my life have I met up with such poverty stricken humans. I'll always remember their faces and homes."[9] In contrast, they had dinner with John Paul Sycip, business entrepreneur, "probably one of the wealthiest Chinese in Manila", and visited the Vargas home which was "beautiful and equipped with thousands and thousands of dollars worth of furniture."[10]

The team did not schedule games on Sundays. Instead the day was packed with ministry. On their first Sunday, they conducted a service at 9:45 AM, held two services in the afternoon, and finished with an outdoor meeting at 7:45 PM.[11]

The team left Manila and traveled south where they made stops in Iloilo, Cebu, Dumaguete, and Bacolod. Jacobsen wrote of his first day in Iloilo, "Between 7:00 and 9:00 AM, I walked around the Iloilo city market where I finally got my eyes opened to some of the pagan conditions of the world." In the afternoon some of the team members went to "the Huk [landless peasants] camp to see a cock fight which was very interesting."[12]

Some of the courts they played on were a far cry from Rizal Coliseum in Manila. On one occasion they arrived at a large high school to play an early morning game only to discover that the dirt court was "muddy because of the rain." Later that day they traveled forty miles by bus over rough country roads to a city which was "really in the sticks." They played a game there before a crowd of 3000. This turned out to be a very rewarding experience because it was an area which missionaries had been unable to penetrate successfully. Jacobsen wrote, "We thank the Lord for allowing us to enter and help spread the Gospel."[13]

Their well-established practice of conducting a half-time program and enrolling people in a Bible study course was occasionally challenged in the Philippines. *The Manila Times* reported that "the thirty minute biblical session during intermission, a regular part of the Christian five's itinerary may not be employed tonight."[14] Jacobsen's diary confirms that this was the case. He reports that after the game played against the Far Eastern University on June 20 the team members "all went to the park across the street from the Manila hotel where they held a meeting consisting of singing and testimonies and passed out enrollment forms urging people to sign up for a Bible correspondence course."[15]

They continued with half time programs at games played away from Rizal Coliseum. On June 24 they played an early morning game at a Chinese high school where Jacobsen spoke through an interpreter for the first time. Later in the day the team traveled to Fort McKinley for a game against an army team. Jacobsen reports that they "sang and distributed their picture" urging the audience members to sign up for the Bible correspondence course. About 600 of the 1500 present signed the forms.[16] On June 26 they played the University of the Philippines on their campus and "during the half time told them of Jesus Christ and passed out our pictures." Approximately 2500 students returned the forms requesting the Bible correspondence course.[17] On the same day the team returned to Rizal Coliseum where they "held a basketball clinic, played an exhibition game along with testimonies, and had special music." About 4000 people attended this

event, the first of its kind to be held in this venue.[18]

The team continued the winning tradition established by the first 1952 VV squad. Some games were easy romps such as against the University of the Philippines in which the final tally was 91-65. Other games were much closer, for example, one played against Far Eastern University in which the final score was 62-61. They lost one game out of the Rizal series to the PRISCO All Stars, 60-53. However, the VV team came back to win the second contest against PRISCO 56-54.

On July 17, the VV team left Manila bound for Taipei. Jacobsen reports that "a large group saw them off including the Sycips" The plane landed in Taiwan at 11:30PM and they were greeted by a number of Christian people. Madame Chiang's personal secretary presented Bonnie Odle and Alice Schaeffer with flowers (see photo on page 112).[19] The following day the cagers held a press conference where photographs were taken and Coach Odle was interviewed. In its July 18 edition *The China News* reported on the team's arrival characterizing various team members and their basketball prowess. Forrest Jackson was dubbed "the tap-in expert", Bud Schaeffer identified as the "iron guard", Howard Habegger described as one to "never say die", Floyd Habick called "the skyscraper", and Don Odle "fleet-footed and jovial." Odle was quoted as saying, "the team is stronger than last year" because they have "the best old guard and have added new first rate sharpshooters."[20]

The first game was played that evening at an army camp where the team had its first encounter with the Chinese cultural value of "saving face." Jacobsen noted:

> Formosa and the people seem to be different [from the Filipinos]. The men at the camp gave their utmost attention as we preached the gospel. They clapped as we entered the ball court. The captain asked us not to run the score up which was done to save face.[21]

The *China News* reported on this first game as follows: "The Youth for Christ Cagers required only a fraction of their prowess and skill to resoundingly beat the young Lang Sheng quintet of Taiwan 86-56 last night in their debut game watched by 5000 fans." The article described outstanding plays by Forrest Jackson, Bud Schaeffer, Jerry Carey, and Paul Hoffman but Odle got the most attention for his "Harlem Globetrotter type one man show." Odle amused the crowd by "scoring on a dead run... making underhand shootings, and by passing the ball back between his two short legs."[22]

The games that VV played in Taiwan varied in the number of spectators and conditions. Some contests such as the one played against the police academy involved relatively few spectators. There were about 700 students present, but during the service after the game an impressive 250 men responded to the invitation. This contest was played early in the morning. The game that evening was a very different experience. The team met the Seven Tigers in the Armed Forces Stadium with 8000 people in attendance.[23] They returned to this stadium again on July 24 to play "the best team in Formosa, the Chinese All Stars." The stadium was full and the lead changed several times during the game.

"Unbelievable" Bud Schaeffer

The Chinese All Stars led at the half but the Americans had "a pair of excellent guards who can be relied on to turn the table on the opponents when the moment seems darkest to the preaching players from Indiana... The Christians came from behind to lead at the close of the third and coasted to their narrowest victory in Taiwan when the final score, 58-51, was announced."[24]

The fourth game played in the Taipei Stadium was marred when a significant group of people became angry with the referees. The contest was halted for a half hour because the crowd was throwing empty bottles, paper balls, and other objects on to the court while shouting for the dismissal of the offending referees. *The China News* noted, "Last night's incident demonstrated one glaring fact: while the standard of basketball players has improved during the past year, many spectators have made no efforts to keep up with the progressive pace in changing their chauvinistic attitude." Despite these problems, the VV team went on to win the game 73-63 largely as a result of Bud Schaeffer's stellar performance. He "foiled many a Chinese fast breaks and managed to get 20 points." Forrest Jackson and Paul Hoffman were also high scorers.[25]

On Tuesday, July 21, the VVers "experienced one of the most thrilling parts of the trip," having lunch with Madame Chiang and her prayer group. Jacobsen reported that his "first impression of her was higher than he had anticipated." At the close of the formal meeting, Madame Chiang spoke to the group praising the 1953 VV team for the work they did, especially the sincerity with which they shared their faith. During lunch, the team members talked with Madame Chiang. Schaeffer asked her about her own faith. Madame answered by describing her experience in China before 1949. She said this experience caused her to "understand more than ever before as her back was to the wall, there was something greater than herself, a man who was as close to her as a brother and a person who would watch over her as she walked with Him day by day."[26] Certainly this type of contact

Crusading Cagers: 1953-1957

President and Madame Chiang Kai-shek with the VV team and missionaries

with world leaders could not help but exert a powerful influence on these young men. In Jacobsen's words, "It was a blessed sight to see the wives of the leaders of Free China gather to seek God's guidance."[27]

As impressive as it was, this meeting with Madame and her prayer group was not the last contact the team had with the country's leaders. On August 7, they traveled to Chiang Kai-shek's home located outside Taipei on Green Mountain. Here they had dinner with President and Madame Chiang. During the Chinese style dinner, toasts were exchanged. Dick Hillis expressed the team's appreciation to their hosts, promising continued support and prayer for them and the people of Nationalist China. Chiang responded by thanking the team and assuring them they would be remembered in prayer as they left Taiwan. Jacobsen reported that he sat between Madame and the President during dessert and aided by an interpreter carried on a conversation with Chiang. He summed up his impressions of the President with this assessment: Chiang is "a very gracious, sincere, humble, but stern man, and most of all a believer in Jesus Christ."[28]

Meeting important government leaders was not the only way the team encountered world politics. They also were exposed to the reality of war. One day several team members accompanied Madame Chiang's pastor to an army hospital where a group of wounded soldiers had just arrived. They visited all of the wards passing out tracts to the wounded men. This was an emotionally overwhelming experience. Jacobsen wrote, "I saw things I'll never forget... War, War... There were those without hands and feet... My prayer is that God will never let me forget what I saw on Friday July 24."[29]

While they were in Taiwan the team was introduced to the behind the scenes organization which made the experience work. They went to Norm Cook's home and saw the compound where Dick Hillis and other missionaries lived. They were given a tour of the offices where the Bible correspondence courses were compiled and mailed. The efficiency of the follow up work deeply impressed the team members.[30]

On July 26 Odle and the team departed Taipei by train for the south of Taiwan. This turned out to be an especially grueling part of the trip. It was extremely hot. They played three games a day beginning at 8:00 in the morning, and they sometimes did not have adequate food and water.[31] Their first destination was Miaoli where they had arranged to stay with a group of indigenous people. From Miaoli they went to Taichung. The train was jammed with people and they "were ushered into the baggage car and sat on mail the entire way." They played two games in Taichung the day they arrived and two more the following day, all at various army camps.[32] The next place to be visited was Chiag-i. Again they found themselves in the baggage car. When they arrived, they were taken to a Japanese style hotel where they slept on "wooden beds" and "the wash stand was in the center of the hotel. It was a real experience."[33] Their final stop was Tainan where they stayed in another Japanese style hotel, sleeping on tatami mats.

The experiences in the cities and rural areas of the southern part of Taiwan deepened their appreciation of the complex culture of the island with its variety of ethnic peoples and traditions. It also brought them face to face with the sometimes difficult reality of the missionaries' lives. During this time they met a number of missionaries, some of whom had been on the Mainland before the Communist takeover. These missionaries often hosted the team for meals, and in return the team visited orphanages, sang at vacation Bible school sessions, and gave their testimonies at church services.[34] This exchange further cemented the strong relationship between the VV teams and career missionaries that continues to characterize sports evangelism to the present time.

Entering Uncharted Regions

The third country visited by this VV team was Japan where they won all the scheduled contests. Upon their arrival, they were met by several Christian leaders including Ted Engstrom and taken to their Tokyo hotel. The team members were struck by the fact that less than a decade after the end of World War II Japan was again becoming a thriving country. Jacobsen wrote

Ted Engstrom (left) and other Christian leaders welcoming the team to Japan

about his first impressions of Japan as follows: "As I turned the first corner I saw smokestacks, people at work, not using man power alone but machines. Tokyo, which was 85% destroyed during the war, has built up like a modern metropolis."[35] They played their first game against Tokyo Education University. A Tokyo newspaper gave this account of the contest.

> The fast breaking, sharp shooting Youth for Christ basketball team made an impressive Japan debut by outclassing the national collegiate champion, The Tokyo Education University squad, 113-84... From a few seconds after the opening tip off when Howdy [sic] Habegger scored a short shot to the final whistle, the American team completely dominated the game... Forrest Jackson with 24 points and Bud Schaeffer with 22 were high point men and standouts for the winners... Among the dignitaries attending was Prince Takamatsu, Chairman of the international good will series.[36]

Introducing the new uniform

Crusading Cagers: 1953-1957

An important feature that contributed to the credibility of these early VV teams was the fact that Odle made official contact with the host country's athletic association. It was probably this connection that led to the opportunities to play some of the best teams in East Asia. The morning after their first game in Japan the team was hosted by the Athletic Association of the city of Niigata, and on Wednesday they were luncheon guests of the Athletic Association of Japan. Prince Takamatsu and his wife were also guests at

Competing at the Korakuen Ice Palace, Tokyo

this event.[37] The team played several more games in various cities including Nagoya, Osaka, and Kyoto. Some of the most important contests were played in the Korakuen Ice Palace in Tokyo with a seating capacity of some 4000. Their last game was played here against the All-Japan team and was televised.[38]

Perhaps the most fortuitous event for the team in

Japan was meeting with Lieutenant General William K. Harrison. In 1951 he was deputy commander of the Eighth Army in Korea and later chief-of-staff for General Mark Clark's Far East and United Nations commands. As leader of the United Nations truce delegation in 1952, he signed the armistice with the North Koreans. Harrison characterized himself "as a sinner saved by grace" who believed that the best hope for the world was Jesus Christ.[39] As a result of this meeting, General Harrison provided Odle with a letter (military type order) which allowed the VV team to move freely in Korea, their next destination.[40]

VV with Lieutentant General William K. Harrison

Korea - 1953

On August 24, shortly after the truce had been declared, the team flew from Tokyo to Pusan, landing on an army airfield where they were given a small reception and interviewed by the press. It was immediately apparent that "the army and war was very near." The team was taken by car from the airport into the city. "The roads were rough, sights were horrible," observed Jacobsen. "One of the worst feelings I've had since we left the US was when we drove along the roads seeing the poverty stricken people... pushing them off the road for a bunch of American basketball players."[41]

They left Pusan immediately on a single car gasoline driven train. The seats were small and "the springs were poking through the upholstery." They rode through the night sleeping little, and arrived in Seoul at 7:30 AM. That day they played "two hard games against two good teams."[42] The following day they played two more games against the Republic of Korea army teams and then left by train for Taijon. They arrived there at 2:15AM and were greeted by a band playing and presented flowers. That night they slept in a tent on army cots.[43]

Musical presentation in a bombed out school in South Korea

The next day they played a game in the rain before a crowd of 5000. They then journeyed to Taigu where they played another game before an audience of 14,000, "the largest crowd ever in two years."[44] Emotionally and physically, Korea exacted a serious toll on the Americans. In two days they had played five games without eating a proper meal. For Jacobsen it was a low point. He wrote:

This evening after the game was over, I walked away from the crowd just to get away from people and be by myself. Five different individuals walked up to me and asked questions during the post-game service. This is a typical experience as we've learned that one of the hardest things we have to do all the time is be on exhibition. Receptions, dinners, banquets, speeches, etc. One almost needs a false personality.[45]

On August 29 the team played their last game, number 82, against an all-Korea squad in Pusan, and then departed for Tokyo. VV had won 81 games, lost 1, traveled 42,000 miles, and witnessed to over 240,000 people in four months. Jacobsen wrote, "The Lord seemed to know about how many games we could play because most of the guys were just about dead after the game."[46]

Not only had the 1953 team successfully re-enforced the strong ties forged in 1952 with the Philippines and the Republic of China, but also had expanded its influence to Japan and South Korea. The extensive press coverage indicated that VV's skills and Christian commitment were now recognized by a wider audience.

Rest and Re-invigoration – 1955-57

No team went to East Asia in 1954 but VV was not forgotten. In that year Coach Odle was burdened by many Taylor responsibilities including directing the athletic program, coaching, speaking, and dealing with problems created by personnel changes. He also wanted to be able to spend time with his family. Odle continued to tell the successful story of Venture for Victory to numerous church and civic groups, and by the spring of 1955 plans were again being made for a trip to East Asia. Hawaii, South Korea, Taiwan, Japan, the Philippines, Hong Kong, and Thailand were on the projected itinerary. Players came from Westmont College, Southern California University and Anderson College.

Bob Culp from Anderson was the first African-American player on a VV team; he hailed from Philadelphia. To his great credit, Coach Odle never showed partiality with respect to a player's ethnic or racial background. In fact, in 1954 Odle as Taylor University's athletic director encouraged Coach Don Granitz to take the College football team to Nashville, Tennessee to play a historically African-American academic institution, Fisk University, at its homecoming. This was the first inter-racial football game played in the State of Tennessee. Taylor won the game 32-0 thanks to halfback Don Callan's four touchdowns.

Bob Culp with admirers

Callan was one of three Taylor University players who were on the 1955 VV team. He grew up in Bright, Indiana, a small town near the Ohio border. He first learned about Taylor at the little Methodist church in that community. Several of the young people from this congregation were enrolled at Taylor and would occasionally bring other Taylor students home on weekends. Callan enrolled at Taylor in the fall of 1951 in order to play football. His experience with high school athletics had largely been in basketball, but he was brash enough to believe "he could do anything" including football. Callan remembers how he arrived for practice and "did not know how to put on the football equipment," but he was "the fastest man on the field when the team ran wind sprints." This caused Coach Odle to "pay attention" to him, and he played his first game against Earlham College just fourteen days later. He lettered three years in both football and basketball, and was voted all conference halfback in 1953 and 1954. His record in Taylor

Don Callan

football was stellar, earning 97 points, the highest in Indiana and fourth in the nation during the 1954 season. He also set the Taylor single game scoring record of four touchdowns.[47]

Callan had applied to go on the 1953 VV trip, but had not been selected. However, he was successful in 1955. Like the members of previous teams, he participated in fund raising activities but received no formal orientation before boarding the trans-Pacific flight, the first of his life.

Ken Stark was a track and basketball player. He was a member of the cross country team, was high hurdles conference champion, and played four years of varsity basketball, the only Taylor player who could have played all five positions on the floor effectively. Joe Grabill came from Converse, Indiana and as a student at Taylor was actively involved in musical ensembles. He was selected to participate on the 1956 team to Latin America and again in 1957 to East Asia.

The 1955 tour began in Japan. Callan relates that numerous sensations bombarded the team when they deplaned in Tokyo. Much to their amazement,

Crusading Cagers: 1953-1957

Acknowledging Japanese fans

they discovered that they literally towered over their Japanese hosts. When they were taken to their accommodations, a traditional ryokan, they discovered that much of Japanese life centered on the tatami-covered floors. Despite suffering from the effects of jetlag, the American cagers were spirited away to play their first game. They soon found themselves in a packed stadium where the crowd was "electric." That night the VV team discovered the Japanese athletes were intensely competitive. Speed and agility made up for their lack of height. Callan recalled they "played the number one team in the nation and it really extended [us] big time."[48]

Later that summer, just two years after the cease fire, they journeyed to South Korea. Two

Ken Stark with young Korean admirers

129

COACH ODLE'S FULL COURT PRESS

Seoul, South Korea

games were particularly memorable. One was played in Seoul in an outdoor stadium which seated over 30,000 people. "I [Callan] played first half. I was kind of rough and tumble and all over the court, diving for balls... 'Coach' said, 'Hey, they are going to love you Don. You give a testimony at half.' I remember standing up and looking at that crowd and saying, 'Wow! Can I do this or not?' But the Lord was good, and we had a number of decisions."[49]

Not all experiences were as exhilarating. The team traveled to Pusan where they played on a makeshift court in a bombed out building dimly lit by four bare bulbs, two over each basket. After the contest, the exhausted players were treated to dinner by the mayor and were elated to discover ice in their soft drinks. A few hours later their elation turned to misery when

Crusading Cagers: 1953-1957

they all became violently ill as they traveled by train across Korea. Their discomfort was magnified when they discovered that all the bathrooms were nonfunctional. It was a long night and the team was unable to play for several days.

Korea was not the only politically unstable area in the mid-1950s. The netmen also felt the ubiquitous military presence in Taiwan. "There were soldiers everywhere. The entrances to stadiums were guarded and people were made to walk single file through the gates."[50]

Since basketball was the national sport in Taiwan, fan loyalty was always at a high fever pitch. Callan recalled one game when the rambunctious crowd became angry at the referees and began to pelt the court with an assortment of objects. The match was halted until a zealous official took control of the public

Playing in a rainstorm in Taiwan

address system and declared, "there are communists in this crowd throwing bottles, and if they are found they will be shot!" The crowd quieted instantly and play resumed.[51]

In a July 1955 prayer letter Schaeffer indicated that the team played two games and sometimes three nearly every day before crowds averaging over 4000. He went

1955 VV team at halftime. Left to right: Jack Mount, Don Callan, Joe Grabill, Tine Hardeman, Ken Stark

on to describe one particular contest played before over 5000 soldiers of the First Armored Division. After the game about 250 men made a commitment to follow Christ. "As we were leaving, one colonel told us he had found the Lord in the summer of 1953 at Feng Shan, the West Point of Formosa, along with 326 others, who had also made decisions. Then he led his wife

132

and children to Christ, and all of them have now completed the Bible correspondence course."[52]

After playing in Taiwan the team went on to Hong Kong, Bangkok, Thailand and the Philippines. In Bangkok, Schaeffer noted that the team had "one of its most fruitful weeks in the Orient...over 200 students in schools made decisions for Christ."[53] The team had planned to go on to Saigon, but this leg of the tour was cancelled because of political unrest.

The VV squad arrived in Manila on August 1. As in previous years, the Philippine media gave extensive coverage to the squad, frequently identifying it as a Taylor University team. The *Manila Times* greeted them with the headline, "Taylor U debuts against PAL tonite." The article reported that "the curtains go up on American 'hoophetry' with a biblical touch tonight at the Rizal Coliseum."[54] The first of a six game series in Manila was played before a small crowd of about 700. The score was 67-53 favoring the VV team. The *Manila Times* dramatized the plight of the Philippine team: "A short, stubby Philippine Air Lines quintet that offered only one six-footer climbed Hoophet's sacrificial altar last night and with bowed heads submitted to the towering Taylor U Trojans." The press focused on Bob Culp as the game's high scorer.[55]

The second Manila game was played against the YCO Painters, the Philippine national champion team. The Painters had obtained permission to import from another team Carlos Loyzaga "a whirling powerhouse who earned international letters in last year's world basketball championship in Brazil"[56] Loyzaga's presence did indeed make a difference as the VV team went down to defeat 61-58. The Manila fans were jubilant over this victory for their local players. The *Times* put it this way:

> Hosannas were heaped on the YCO Painters last night... The choir was a highly partial throng of 7,000 that roared itself hoarse as the Painters battled the towering statesiders for 37 minutes and then broke through with flourish in the retiring moments.[57]

The high scorer in this game was Tine Hardeman from Westmont College who in following years would return to the Philippines as a missionary and continue to play basketball with VV teams as well as playing on leading Philippine teams.

The third game played in Rizal was against the San Miguel Brewery (SMB) Braves. VV won 87-56. According to the *Manila Times*, "The hoosiers unfolded a smashing all out offensive" sending the nearly 4,000 fans home "wowed by the Trojans' terrific display of speed" but disappointed by the loss.[58] The article was accompanied by a photo showing Ken Stark, Tine Hardeman and Bob Culp preventing an SMB player from shooting. The caption under the picture read: "Ken Stark, Tine Hardeman and Bob Culp of the Taylor U Trojans loom like so many Mt. Everests as they gang up on a marooned Rafael Barretto of San Miguel Brewery at the Rizal Coliseum last night."[59] The high scorer in

Bob Culp being greeted by Philippine President Ramon Magsaysay

this game was once again Tine Hardeman. Most of the articles that appeared in the *Manila Times* focused on the height advantage of the VV players. The members of the team averaged more than six feet in 1955.

The fourth game was played against the Seven-Up Maurauders, winners of the 1955 M.I.C.A.A. championship before a crowd of 9000 in Rizal Coliseum. VV won this game 63-59. The *Manila Times* reported "Taylor U's sharp-shooting Trojans withstood a blazing rally from the Seven-Up Marauders... that added to the axiom of the big man eating up the little man at the Rizal Coliseum."[60]

The last Manila game before the team left for the south was a contest held at the downtown YMCA which VV won 60 to 53. Following the Manila series the *Manila Times* reported on VV's travel plans to "start an extensive 'preach and pray' tour." VV won all thirteen games played during this tour.[61]

The final game the 1955 VV team played was against the Seven-Up Marauders in Rizal before a crowd of 6000. The headline read "Taylor U beats 7-Up anew, 72-60. Bible-preaching cagers post 6th Manila Victory." The *Manila Times* reported: "Taylor U's Trojans wrote the last page in their tour of the Far East last night with a convincing 72-60 walloping of the Seven-Up Marauders in their return bout."[62] Culp was the high scorer in the game. Norm Cook was reported as praising the Marauders despite the lopsided score. "They're the best balanced team you have... Good sports, good stamina, good plays... Without Loysaga for Yco, Seven-Up is a very much better team."[63]

By the end of the summer, the players were exhausted. In two and a half months, they had played 59 games, winning 57, and conducted 210 evangelistic meetings along the way. This impressive record was achieved in spite of Odle's back problem which necessitated his early departure for home, Bud Schaeffer's appendectomy, and Jack Mount's serious ankle injury. Fortunately the team was under the capable leadership of Norm Cook.

Despite the hectic schedule and the hardships, the team never wavered from its primary objective, using sports to evangelize. A typical experience was the one encountered during a game in Taiwan. On this occasion Bud Schaeffer preached at halftime. At the game's conclusion, he encouraged those who wanted to know more about Christ to remain. Callan remembered everyone remained after the game. "No one budged." The team remained for a considerable amount of time "trying to deal with people because they were so hungry for what the Gospel presented to them. It was a tremendous time."[64]

Branching Out - 1956

The first three trips to East Asia had demonstrated the powerful potential for evangelizing by combining the energy of young college athletes with the commitment of career missionaries. Odle's instinctive choice of Norm Cook, a Taylor alumnus working in East Asia, as his primary contact had proven to be extremely effective. By 1956 Odle was ready for a new challenge leading him to enlarge the VV program by focusing on an entirely new area of the world, Latin America. This was a ground breaking experience, but not as well organized as the two previous experiences in East Asia. Another factor that made the trip difficult was that soccer was the most popular sport in South America and basketball had not been fully developed.[65] Despite difficulties the team jelled and the players expressed satisfaction at being part of the team.

The catalyst for this trip was another Taylor alumnus, Don Granitz, who had recently taken up his responsibilities as a missionary in Brazil. Granitz had been a member of the first VV team and this experience enabled him to plan the itinerary and make the necessary connections with missionaries and basketball teams. Granitz arranged a schedule which included Guatemala, Ecuador, Peru, Brazil, Colombia,

Crusading Cagers: 1953-1957

The 1956 team. Taylor students included Habegger (second from right) and Grabill (right)

and Venezuela, but the longest time was spent in Brazil where they played 25 games. The team was undefeated in nearly 60 contests. Ken Stark, Joe Grabill, Howard Habegger and Granitz represented Taylor with other players coming from Hope College, Wheaton College, Seattle Pacific College, Biola College, Anderson College, and Stanford University.

The team members began their experience on Taylor's campus where they practiced together. They then drove to Miami. Clyde Cook from Biola (its current president) remembers the emotional pain of witnessing discrimination in the South against Bob Culp, an African American player from Anderson College. Because he was frequently denied service in southern restaurants, it was necessary to bring his food to the car.

The team flew from Miami to South America. Their arrival in Quito, Ecuador occurred only a few months after the highly publicized martyrdom of five missionaries who had attempted to make the first contact with

137

the Auca Indian tribe in the eastern part of the country. The VV team stayed in the missionary compound where they met Elizabeth Elliot and Marge Saint the widows of Jim Elliot and Nate Saint, two of the five martyred men. Cook recalls the team was invited by Marge Saint to her home for a meal. Her young son, Steve, showed Cook the spear with which his father had been killed. Steve said, "Jesus must have loved Daddy more than me because he got to see him first."[66] That moving experience had a great influence on Cook's thinking.

The Americans were well received in Ecuador, and the games went well. In Peru and Colombia it

Coach Odle with Brazilian friends

was a different story. The team arrived in Lima during a time of great social turmoil. Colombia was difficult because there was considerable opposition from the Roman Catholic Church towards Protestants, and political violence had erupted in Bogota the week before the team arrived. Odle said, "This was one of the few times I've been scared. I thought someone was going to put a knife in my back."[67] One game was played in a very large bull fighting arena and the crowd was not receptive to the half time program. However, Odle remembers that after the game at least one man did respond positively by seeking more information about the Gospel.

Brazil was much more receptive to the VV team than Peru and Colombia. Three weeks were spent in this country playing in smaller cities traveling extensively by bus on roads covered with fine red dust. Cook recalls a humorous incident when a Brazilian star player kept appearing at various contests, always greeted prior to the game by young women carrying bouquets of roses. No roses were forthcoming for the VV team! As far as Cook was concerned, the most important event in Brazil occurred one night when it was his turn to give the half time sermonette. For some ten minutes Cook described "his friend" who had done so much for him including laying down his own life. Then Cook revealed his friend—Jesus Christ. At that point the entire crowd rose in their places and cheered. "It was incredible. There was just something about that crowd and I had them with me!" [68]

Odle recalled that on one occasion he and Don Granitz were flying over the Brazilian jungle when the pilot lost his way. At the time both of their wives were pregnant and the two men entertained each other by imagining that even if they did not return from this jungle plane ride, they might each have a son and the boys would grow up, become basketball players and attend Taylor together. Of course, the men did return from the trip but their fantasy came true in part—their wives both gave birth to daughters, who grew up, came to Taylor and participated in sports! In fact, Odle had to fly home in the middle of the summer because Bonnie was having serious difficulties with her pregnancy. This left Granitz in charge of the team for the remainder of the trip which ended in Venezuela.

venture for victory 4

Basketballs and Bibles in South America

139

COACH ODLE'S FULL COURT PRESS

Cook remembers a mix up in the team's schedule in Venezuela. The squad flew to Caracas with suitcases filled with three weeks worth of laundry. When they arrived they learned that the YFC missionaries were not yet ready for them so they packed up their dirty laundry and flew on to Maracaibo. However, there was no one there to meet them either. Finally a missionary did come to take them to their accommodations. To everyone's consternation, the team had been provided with one way tickets to Maracaibo! Someone would have to find the money for their return ticket to Caracas. David Howard, Elisabeth Elliot's brother, was a missionary in Colombia and was in Maracaibo at the time. He gathered the team together and they prayed earnestly for funds. But Howard also prayed that some of the team members would be led to consider mission work as their future vocation. Cook remembers that the necessary funds materialized and years later half the team including Cook did go on to mission work.[69]

Return to Familiar Territory - 1957

Even though the 1956 team had enjoyed some success, particularly in Brazil, Odle was not totally convinced that Latin America was open to an evangelically oriented basketball team at that point. The facilities were not always appropriate and the crowds in some locations were not responding positively to the team's evangelistic message. Therefore, in 1957 Venture for Victory returned to East Asia where VV had an established support in Orient Crusades and they knew that the fans would be receptive to basketball. However, basketball was changing in East Asia. The teams were more competitive and VV was often pitted against professional squads with taller more experienced players.

Taylor's Joe Grabill and George Glass participated on the 1957 team. Other players on this team came

140

Crusading Cagers: 1953-1957

from Wheaton (Dick Kamm), Biola (Clyde Cook), Anderson (Gary Ausbun) and Spring Arbor (Fred Whims). Bud Schaeffer, Don Ulrich, Bill McKee and Norm Cook all Orient Crusades missionaries also joined the cagers. Because Odle had back problems he did not go on the trip, but he continued his responsibilities as director of the program.

It is evident the choice of young men to play on VV teams was crucial. Since Odle could take only a few Taylor athletes, he tended to select those with whom he had developed a strong relationship beyond the basketball court. George Glass whose relationship with Odle began when the latter recruited him for Taylor was such an individual.

Glass was raised in Alexandria, Indiana, the youngest of four children born to godly parents who had not attended college. He was a basketball star in high school, and he sang in a quartet which included Bill Gaither who has become a popular Christian song writer and musician. Glass was preparing to enroll at Anderson College but he came to Taylor University in the summer of 1954 to meet Coach Odle who would be of enormous importance to this young high school athlete. Glass remembers that the day he visited "Coach", Taylor's Maytag Gym had a strong animal smell, and the floor was covered with straw because the recreation class had held its annual county fair in the gymnasium that weekend! Odle persuaded Glass to consider applying to Taylor, and his parents were thrilled when he decided to come. He had strayed from Christianity and perhaps, they thought, he might rediscover his faith at this college.[70]

Glass recalls that because the VV program was "so unique", it was "the

George Glass

141

COACH ODLE'S FULL COURT PRESS

talk of the [Taylor] campus, and he was thrilled to be chosen to play guard on the 1957 team." Preparing for departure was a busy time because $2000 per player had to be raised to pay for the tour. Odle "relentlessly" went from church to church and town to town speaking on behalf of VV and Taylor University, and encouraging people to give financially to the summer ventures. "Coach" would finish basketball practice and take a quick shower, frequently neglecting to eat an evening meal. He and a student driver—sometimes Glass—would jump into Odle's car and head for a meeting somewhere in Indiana, Ohio or Michigan. Glass recalls Odle would ask him to stop so that they could purchase a six pack of Coca Cola. Glass asserted, "He lived on cokes!"[71] Jay Kesler, another student driver, remembers that Odle loved kosher corn beef sandwiches along with his cokes. In fact, Odle introduced Kesler to this delicacy.[72] After a speaking engagement, Odle was so wound up that he would drive for awhile. Becoming exhausted, he would ask Glass to take the wheel so he could get some rest. "Odle worked harder than anyone; he poured himself into everything", recalls Glass.

The 1957 tour began in Taiwan on June 22 and then continued on to Hong Kong, Thailand, Singapore and Indonesia. The longest stop was in the Philippines where the team played from July 26 to August 20. The Americans went undefeated in 70 games.

The team was met in Taipei by Norm Cook. Even though the VV players were tired from their long journey, Cook immediately got them involved in a scrimmage in preparation for the first evening's contest against the Chinese Olympic team which was to be played before over 12,000 excited fans. Clyde Cook remembers VV was four points down in the last few minutes. "We thought we were cooked!" This would have been the first time any VV team would have lost in Taiwan. But to everyone's surprise VV ended up winning by one point. The next night they again played the Olympic team and won by a close three point margin.

Crusading Cagers: 1953-1957

The third night history repeated itself when VV met the Chinese Olympic team and won by one point. The local newspaper came out the next day with the headline, "It's not fair! God helped them win!"[73]

VV and Chinese Olympic team

The following Sunday Clyde Cook preached in a local church. After the service a young boy who had been at the third game with his mother came down to talk with him. Cook, along with the Chinese pastor and a missionary, were invited to come to their home and meet an older son. The family was interested in hearing more about the Christian faith. Cook did not know where to begin talking about his faith but he asked the eldest son, "What do you know about Jesus Christ?" The young man answered, "Who is he?" Cook remembered he had heard missionaries tell about people who had not heard about Christ, but he personally had never had this experience. Cook started with Genesis and spent about an hour explaining the Bible. "When I got through I asked them if they would like to become children of God. They said yes, and we prayed together." As Cook left the young man held his hand all the way down the stairs and thanked him profusely for introducing him to Jesus. As Cook was riding back to the hotel in a pedicab he decided that he wanted "to spend the rest of his life winning people to Jesus." Cook kept in touch with the young man and learned that in subsequent months twenty-seven members of his family had become believers.[74] Glass recalls the experience in East Asia as "the hardest period of nine weeks I have ever had in my life."[75]

Philippines 1957

As was the case in many of these trips, the Philippines was last on the itinerary. Basketball was "king" in this country and the local press was particularly interested in running detailed stories on the VV team. The netmen arrived in Manila from Jakarta, Indonesia, and they were scheduled to play a total of 40 games in Manila and in the provinces. Interviewed at the airport, Bud Schaeffer said they were "looking forward to tough opposition in the Philippines". Joe Grabill who participated in both Latin America and East Asia noted in an interview with the *Manila Times* reporter that the best teams he competed against were in Brazil and the Philippines.[77]

VV played several games prior to their first big clash with a M.I.C.A.A. team at Rizal Coliseum. In each of these exhibition games they "fashioned out one-sided" victories.[78] The first M.I.C.A.A. team to be taken on was the Yellow Taxi which had made a good showing in the recently completed league tournament partly due to the fact that it had several tall players. As in previous years the issue of the height difference between the American and Philippine players was often raised in newspaper reports. The July 30 *Manila Times* reported on this first Rizal game under the headline "Taylor U beats Yellow Taxi, 83-62" The lead sentence proclaimed, "Basketball's bible-preaching powerhouse crew, the Taylor U Trojans, served their first dish of power basket-

Crusading Cagers: 1953-1957

ball at the Rizal Coliseum last night by running rough-shod over the Yellow Taxi Cabbies, 83-62." Ironically the high scorer for VV was Gary Ausbun, the only team member under six feet! "The Trojans...set a torrid fire-house pace ...letting loose barrage after barrage from all angles," reported *The Manila Times*.[79] Unfortunately, Clyde Cook suffered a bad sprain in his left foot after falling during the fourth quarter, an injury which kept him from returning to the court that season.

Interviewed after the game, Norm Cook said, "I wish we can win all these games, but if we should lose, we would rather lose here than in any other place. You've got good clubs here."[80] Cook's winning wish came true as their "pressing man to man guard-ing" enabled them to achieve a clean sweep of their six contests in Rizal Coliseum.[81]

The two games between VV and the YCO Painters created great excitement among the fans. YCO was "the only Filipino team that has beaten the powerful Americans" in their previous trips to Manila. The first of two games between these two teams was played on August 9 before 8000 fans, "the biggest crowd yet drawn by the Trojans at the Coliseum."[82] Much to the disappointment of the crowd, the YCOans star, Carlos Loyzaga, was not playing and the VV team won hand-ily with an eleven point margin. Ten days later the two squads met again. This time Loyzaga was back with them "to fortify the Painters attempt to vindicate their 87-76 defeat."[83] But even Loyzaga could not achieve the much desired victory, and the game ended with another VV win. The *Manila Times* lead paragraph told the story. "Local hoopdom's No. 1 squad, the YCO Painters, went down again before Taylor U's tireless Trojans last night in a bristling rematch that practi-cally sealed the American's bid to perfect a 72 game winning streak this year." The game was played before a standing room crowd of 12,000 people.[84]

Two other games were particularly memorable because the VV team barely won after tense hard fought contests. They were the games against 7-Up and Crispa. The *Manila Times* declared, "Marauders [7-Up] scare V-for-V quintet in second half. Silva's bottlers force bible-preaching Americans to freeze ball in closing minutes." After declaring that the VV team would surely be desirous of a return match, the article went on to note "...the Marauders almost slapped the law of averages on Norman Cook's 'moiderous' V-for-V huskies last night in slugging it out and forcing them to settle for their narrowest winning margin yet, 63 to 61."[85] Schaeffer fouled out early in the second half giving the Marauders an edge. In a post game interview, Norm Cook said, "We found it hard without him [Schaeffer]...but that team turned out to be stronger than we expected. Great squad. They played very smart basketball—they know how to play against tall opponents...[we] had a hard match in Formosa, but this is the closest, the most tense."[86]

The final game of the 1957 tour was played against Crispa-Floro and was a hard fought see-saw contest that VV nearly lost. Although at one point Crispa led 51-43, VV was able to pull ahead and the game ended 64-61. It was VV's 119th consecutive win in two years.

The four years between 1954 and 1957 served to solidify VV's "crusading" reputation. They appeared to their Asian competition, particularly the professional Philippine teams, as nearly invincible on the basketball court.

Crusading Cagers: 1953-1957

美　　國
青年歸主籃球隊

VENTURE
for
VICTORY

四十七年六月廿四日至七月四日

Front page of tracts passed out to
thousands of Chinese in Formosa and
Hong Kong.

Chapter Six

WHAT PRICE GLORY- 1958-1964

By 1958, the fame of VV and Don Odle had spread even to the halls of the U.S. Congress. On February 26 of that year Indiana Congressman John V. Beamer included in the Congressional Record the following remarks:

> Mr. Speaker, in these times when people of good intent are trying to devise new means of helping mankind, it is most encouraging to report the work of one individual in the religious field. Don J. Odle, director of Venture for Victory and director of Athletics at Taylor University, Upland, In. has been taking basketball teams into many foreign countries. Before each game and during halves, Mr. Odle and his athletes chosen from various Indiana [sic] colleges give testimony to their religious faith which they not only profess but also practice.

COACH ODLE'S FULL COURT PRESS

Under unanimous consent, I ask to have placed in the appendix of the Congressional Record the recent news release of Mr. Odle on the next Venture for Victory that has been arranged.[1]

By the late fifties VV teams were known throughout East Asia. The teams commanded the attention of reporters everywhere they went especially in the Philippines. Odle's reputation as an effective coach grew each season until in 1960 he was able to achieve his life long dream of coaching an Olympic team.

The level of competition during this period increased dramatically as VV began playing more and more national Olympic teams. VV's win-loss record remained strong, but they lost more often to these high powered teams. Although VV continued to bear significant Christian witness, there appeared to be a subtle shift towards emphasizing the importance of winning contests. Odle's strategy for selecting players changed. Instead of choosing team members primarily from the Christian college circuit, he began to search for big name Christian players from large universities. By 1964, these trends culminated in major difficulties in the Philippines leading ultimately to a rethinking of VV's mission accompanied by administrative reorganization.

Retaining the Competitive Edge – 1958-1959

In response to the increasing competitiveness and skill of Asian teams, Odle sought to recruit players of national recognition. The 1958 team consisted of nationally known center Ed Beck (6'7") from the University of Kentucky and center Tink Van Patton from Temple University. Beck was the captain of the University of Kentucky basketball team leading them to the National Collegiate championship in 1957. At 6'8" and weighing 235 pounds, Van Patton was the biggest man on the VV squad. He was described as a tremendous rebounder who helped to lead his

What Price Glory — 1958-1964

1958 VV Team

home team to 25 consecutive wins and Temple University's participation in the national championship finals. Guard Jack Mount from the University of Southern California was also selected for a second time. Taylor stars Jack King and Roger Jenkinson were on the team. King, an all round athlete in football, basketball, and baseball, was named Hoosier Conference all Star player, and voted most valuable player on the Taylor Trojan squad. Jenkinson was only 19 years old, the youngest player on any VV squad. He was also the shortest of the 1958 players but he was a tremendous jumper which made up for his lack of height. He had been one of Taylor's leading rebounders and scorers during the 1957-58 season. Jenkinson was not originally selected to go but George Glass suffered a back injury and "Coach" asked Jenkinson to take his place.

Jenkinson played basketball in high school, was interested in continuing to play in college while studying architecture and engineering, and had selected the University of Delaware. But he recalls an athletic banquet in his high school senior year when Coach Odle was the featured speaker. After the banquet, Odle sug-

Roger Jenkinson

151

gested Jenkinson should come to Taylor University and practice with the VV team that was heading to Latin America during the summer of 1956. Jenkinson accepted Odle's invitation, and the experience proved to be a positive one for the young high schooler. He was particularly impressed by the spiritual dedication and athletic skills of these athletes. Odle encouraged Jenkinson to consider coming to Taylor as a student and by the end of the summer he had decided to do just that. Jenkinson played both basketball and baseball as a Taylor student lettering in both sports and was the 1959 Hoosier Conference champion.[2]

Jenkinson recalls Odle devoted the weekends to speaking on behalf of the VV program, sometimes delivering three to four presentations in a single day. Odle recruited students to help him during these weekend trips, and Jenkinson was one of them. He would help with the driving, and when they arrived he would set up the slide projector because every presentation included photographs. After awhile, Jenkinson

1958 team in Vietnam

fondly remembers he had Odle's entire presentation memorized including all the jokes. Even though these talks were liberally sprinkled with humor, the tone became serious, at times even emotional, as Odle appealed to his audience for financial and prayer support for his VV program. Jenkinson noted that the Odles were so dedicated to the cause that at one time they even considered mortgaging their own home in order to raise sufficient funds for the VV teams.[3]

The itinerary for the 1958 VV team began with one week practice in Hawaii. Then the cagers headed for Korea, Japan, Okinawa, Taiwan, Hong Kong, the Philippines, Vietnam, Singapore and the Malayan Peninsula. Jenkinson recalls that the team had it "nice" in comparison to the more rugged conditions of years past, and that Odle always made sure they were well rested and well fed. In Korea, Taiwan, and Vietnam they stayed with missionaries; in Japan and Hong Kong in comfortable hotels; and in Okinawa at a military base.

Jenkinson remembers a number of humorous events involving "Coach" during the summer of 1958. One hilarious incident took place during a televised game at Manila's Rizal Coliseum before some 14,000 people. A seemingly pompous official was assigned the task of shooting off blanks with a pistol to signal the end of play. Excitement was running high at these large Manila games. Odle decided that he should "do something to break the tension that arose each night," and he arranged a rather elaborate joke with one of the fans. His co-conspirator was to place a dead duck on the rafters right above the place where the time keeper would shoot his pistol toward the ceiling to signal the end of the game's first half. As the gun was fired, a string was to be pulled causing the duck to fall at the official's feet. All seemed to be going according to plan except that throughout the game the players were slipping and sliding as water periodically was appearing on the floor. No one could understand why this was happening, but finally the first half ended. The pistol shot was fired and suddenly a strange object plummeted from the rafters landing with a frightening thud near the time keeper. By mistake the fan had placed a frozen duck in the rafters. If it had landed on the referee or anyone else, it could have caused serious bodily injury, and the prank would have been lost.

Odle also enjoyed jokes played on him. He seemed to attract women who preferred passing up the young, virile, handsome players for the "Coach." Jenkinson remembers that when this happened the team would surround Odle so that he could not get away from his admirers. In one incident in the mountains of north-eastern Taiwan, Jenkinson recalls the hot and tired players saw a beautiful stream. Since they were wearing their basketball uniforms they decided to go for a swim. Although "Coach" was not wearing trunks, he decided to join his players in the cool refreshing water clad in his undershorts. In a matter of a few minutes around the curve of the road came a group of Japanese tourists. The VV team ran back to the bus leaving Odle trapped in the water to face the bemused visitors.

Jenkinson recollects that Odle did not like to lose a basketball game. He always remained calm except perhaps when there was a glitch with the scheduling. However, "Coach" never lost sight of the fact that the primary purpose of the tour was for the team to be a Christian witness. Odle's Christian commitment was always "unwavering" and the goal was to win people to Christ. He may not be a theologian, noted Jenkinson, but his message was simple and always on target. "Odle was as straight as a stick. He

"Coach" watching the action

was a showman, he knew how to work people over, he knew how to manipulate people and I mean that in a positive way. But he also knew why we were there..." Jenkinson also commented that "we never, never tried to fool people."[4]

Good sportsmanship was taken seriously and when a player occasionally was carried away by a perceived bad call, the team rallied to calm down the situation. During those early years, the teams were often frustrated by the differences in rules and officiating which they encountered. It was probably to be expected that the officials tended to favor the local team, especially when they pitted their best players against the VV cagers. To their credit, most of the VV teams were able to take these situations in stride by remembering that their real mission was not merely to win basketball games but to be a Christian witness.

However, there was at least one occasion in 1958 in which some members of the VV team appeared to "lose their cool". It occurred the day after they had been to Malacanang Palace to meet President Carlos Garcia. They were playing one of the final games of the 1958 tour in the Philippines where a terrific rivalry had developed over the years. Their opposition was a team billed as the M.I.C.A.A. all stars, a group of the strongest players in the league including Carlos Loyzaga, widely recognized as the best of the best. The all stars were leading by a wide

VV Team with Philippine President Carlos Garcia

155

margin during the game's first half, but during the second half it turned into a bruising duel with one or two points separating the teams. Then with one minute twenty-four seconds left to play, an unfortunate incident occurred. This is the way *The Manila Bulletin* reported the event.

'We wuz robbed!'

That, to put it bluntly, was the sentiment the Taylor U Trojans must have felt last night after the M.I.C.A.A. All-Filipino selection had handed the Venture for Victory cagers their first defeat in 19 starts here this season, a questionable 84-83 decision witnessed by 6,000 fans at the Rizal Memorial Coliseum

And the Trojans had good reason to gripe, at that. The officiating last night seemed a bit too one-sided in favor of the local basketeers....

In summary a foul was comitted against Mount by Loyzaga. But another player, Alfonso Marquez, knowing Loyzaga would be sidelined for keeps unless he did something about it, stretched his arm to take the foul on himself, and scorer Romulo Karganilla, seeing only Marquez's hand upraised, marked down the foul as his.

On the ensuing play, Loyzaga tried a layup of his own, but was fouled by Trojan Bud Schaeffer in the attempt. That foul, although committed on a player who technically had no business being on the court was ruled as Schaeffer's fifth, and the American ordered to the bench.[5]

Jenkinson remembered that Ed Beck became very upset and had to be calmed down by Jack Mount. Jenkinson believes this oversight on the part of the referee enabled the Philippine team to beat the VV squad.[6]

On this occasion, other members of the VV team

were unable to keep from expressing their frustration at this turn of events. Various team members were quoted in the same article when they were interviewed after the game and "spoke freely and heatedly" about their opinion of the officiating referee. Norm Cook who was coaching the team said, "We don't mind losing, but we like to lose fair and square." Schaeffer said that "the officiating was very poor." Ed Beck had the most heated statement of all. "You should bring some good American basketball officials to hold officiating clinics here; your referees just don't know the rules."[7] The incident was widely reported in the Philippine press with varying degrees of sympathy for the VV team

A total of 83 games were played during the 1958 season with 81 wins and 2 losses, 1 in Taiwan and 1 in Manila, both by one point. The last game in Manila was won in triple overtime. In addition, nine basketball clinics were held. There were also 219 meetings (the largest number were in Singapore and Malaya with 62 followed by Hong Kong with 49) besides those held at the games. Over 300,000 people attended these events and nearly 6700 were inquirers in response to the Gospel presentation.[8]

Jenkinson was again selected for the 1959 VV team to East Asia. While he describes the 1958 experience as "fabulous", the second trip was marred by problems and disappointments but still a life changing experience for the participants. The 1959 team included Jenkinson, Schaeffer, Paul Neuman (Stanford University), Bill Gerig and Bob Whitehead both from Wheaton College, and W.A. Preston and E.J. McIlvain from Rice University. Due to recurrent back problems, Odle did not join the team and Norm Cook was assigned the coaching and leadership responsibilities. Jenkinson noted that Cook, being an outstanding missionary, was determined that 1959 would be a mission trip and that the team would live like missionaries. "I [Jenkinson] slept on floors, we had to eat indigenous foods, people would get sick, we would be tired, everybody would be grumbling... That's OK.

COACH ODLE'S FULL COURT PRESS

I learned some things. But I don't think I played my best ball."[9] Jenkinson came home from that summer with a viral infection and suffering from exhaustion. It was a grueling summer because the team frequently played two or three games a day. During the daylight hours there were "pick up" games in the barrios, and at night the more publicized and demanding contests in the large stadiums. Nevertheless the experience greatly impacted the direction of the lives of every player.

A second problem during this seventh VV summer centered around the controversy regarding Bud Schaeffer's former basketball career. M.I.C.A.A. protested that Schaeffer had played professional ball earlier in his career and it, therefore, refused to participate in competition against the VV team. This resulted in sudden changes in the Philippine itinerary. Despite the difficulties, the VV cagers wound up with an impressive 52-1-1 record for the summer.

Team members recall many dramatic experiences during the summers of 1958 and 1959. One night in a large stadium in Taipei Norm Cook dove for a basketball in a particularly competitive contest, and accidentally hit a Taiwanese player. The fans got mad and began throwing mats on which they were sitting onto the court. Fortunately for the players the court was surrounded by a fence. At this point Jenkinson remembers a high ranking general who was at the game taking the microphone. After he had spoken briefly, the situation completely changed. Jenkinson learned afterwards that the general had said in Chinese that "this is communist inspired and the next one throwing mats will be taken to jail." In another tense game in a stadium in Kaoshiung, Taiwan, the crowd was packed so tightly that people spilled onto the court. Eventually there was only a narrow strip between the two goals. The crowd was repeatedly requested to move back, and when they did not comply soldiers with machine guns were brought in. The rest of the game continued with the court surrounded by military personnel.

What Price Glory — 1958-1964

A more humorous situation, Jenkinson recalls, was when the VV cagers played a game in a new stadium in Kuala Lumpur, Malaya. Before the game the janitor waxed the new parquet floor! This presented an unusual challenge to the players when they found themselves sliding over the entire court. In Serambang in the mountains of the central Malayan Peninsula, a game was played before a packed crowd on a court over which hung two long strands of lights. When Jenkinson got a rebound, he had a knack of throwing a football style pass to the other end of the court. On one occasion in the contest, Jenkinson's pass knocked out an entire string of lights accompanied by a loud popping sound. The remainder of the game was played on a half lit court.

The teams traveled by every conceivable means. Probably the most anxious times were on flights in stormy weather. In one particularly hazardous trip, recalls Jenkinson, the team was on a flight over the Pescadores Islands west of Taiwan when the plane caught the edge of a typhoon. The old aircraft had been used as a military plane during World War II and had flown over "the Hump" between India and China. The plane took a sudden dive. Jenkinson remembers seeing its wings flapping up and down in the storm. The aircraft was equipped with six parachutes for 23 passengers who sat on canvas seats. In order to get air, one pulled a cork out of the windows. Nevertheless, the plane was sturdy and eventually landed safely. Jenkinson notes that in the late 1950s he and his colleagues were young and never thought about the dangers that they were actually experiencing.

Every year a high point for the teams was meeting VIPs including Madame Chiang Kai-shek. Jenkinson states that she was "very kind, extremely polite, very happy to have us, very gracious."[10] Her prayer ladies were always eager to support the team.

The players remember the attentiveness of the people as they gave their testimonies at half time. "We were just the draw", commented Jenkinson. The missionaries and local pastors continued what VV had begun. Many times they stood with the players during half time so that the people could more easily identify them. At the completion of a game, the team frequently was "smothered" by people seeking tracts and other Christian literature. The players tried to distribute the materials in an orderly fashion by holding them in the air. But Jenkinson recalls the crowds were so hungry for the leaflets that "they pulled the hair under your arms in order to obtain one." Jenkinson was particularly impressed by the spiritual depth of the Koreans. "We learned a lot from South Koreans because they were very dedicated Christians." South Korea was a difficult place to travel because the after effects of the Korean conflict were still visible in the late 1950s.

Jenkinson also remembers how the missionaries were eager to

Arrival in Korea

show everything to the team members including death houses in Singapore, opium dens in Hong Kong, and leprosariums. One memorable incident for him was visiting a leprosarium in South Vietnam and discovering cats tied to the beds of the lepers. Upon inquiring about this, Jenkinson was told that the cats kept away rodents who otherwise would be attracted by blood from the patients' sores. All of these experiences had a profound impact on the maturation of the young men.

A Dream Comes True - 1960

Odle was selected to be the coach of the 1960 Republic of China's (ROC) Olympic basketball team. This was a great honor for Odle as basketball was Taiwan's most popular sport. Odle notes in *Taylor Made*:

> Childhood dreams sometimes come to fulfillment. From the time I was a small boy, I read stories of and articles about Olympic athletes and their performances. Little did I ever dream that I would have an opportunity to some day participate in one of these colossal, monumental events. The experiences I had in Rome in 1960 while coaching the Chinese Olympic basketball team were a fulfillment of those childhood dreams.[11]

When Odle arrived in Taiwan to begin three months of training with the squad, he was greeted at the airport by the team along with about two hundred people. A large sign read: "WELCOME, MR. ODLE." A press conference was held with about a dozen newspaper reporters. There was a great amount of enthusiasm about the team's possibilities of winning contests in Rome in August.

The Olympic team was composed of twelve men between the ages of 20 and 29. The shortest player was 5' 8" and the tallest about 6' 3", making it the shortest basketball team participating in the summer Olympics. Three of the players were serving in the army, one in the marines and three were college students. There was also a policeman, a school teacher, and a government interpreter. Most of the players had been born on the Mainland and had fled after the 1949 Communist revolution.[12]

1960 Republic of China Olympic team

Odle noted that during the three months of training "we practiced two hours every morning and two hours each evening, the team members learning very fast and being quick to pick up all the drills."[13] Because only some of the players spoke English, there were some language problems. Odle recalled that

> When I said, 'cut' for the basket, some of them thought I meant to go out, get a saw and cut the basket down. They always used the term 'drive.' They did not have the term 'hustle'... They used the term 'ming-ping' which literally meant to 'die for it.'[14]

What Price Glory — 1958-1964

Eighteen exhibition games were scheduled against other All-star and Olympic teams from the Philippines and Japan before the Rome Olympics. In Taipei on Friday, June 24, the team played the first of five exhibition games against Venture for Victory. Odle recounted the excitement generated by these contests.

> Fever and enthusiasm were high, and the game [s] was [were] a complete sellout... A capacity crowd of 8,000 filled the stadium and 3,000 fans mingled on the outside listening to scores over the P.A. system and joining the roar of the crowd... Tickets were scarcer than 'truth at a Summit Conference'... Generals, admirals, senators, and movie stars were among the spectators that crowded into the stadium...[15]

These games were described as "real barn-burners." The audience was thrilled that their team won two of the first four games. Odle described the final contest:

> The last game was a real floor-scorcher that would have left even a Hoosier fanatic limp. The score was tied nine times and the lead changed hands seven times with the VV team always pulling ahead, then being caught and pulling ahead again. With fifty seconds to go, the American team took a four-point lead but the Chinese Olympians caught them with 10 seconds to go only to commit a foul and see Mel Peterson... drop in the winning point. Outside of a few seats being thrown at the umpires and some hisses, it was a pretty orderly game and one which most fans will remember for a long time.[16]

During the next month the enthusiasm on the part of the fans continued to increase. At scrimmage sessions, hundreds and even thousands would turn out to watch the team's workout. "The people cheered whenever a boy executed a play properly and every time I demonstrated something, an audience applause always followed. The problem was this: How can I [Odle] correct a boy for his mistakes in front of two thousand people who believe in face saving?"

COACH ODLE'S FULL COURT PRESS

One of the Olympic leaders felt that these practice sessions should be kept open for the fans. Odle noted,

> Believe me practice never was so important. This thing really boiled down to a Chinese version of a Broadway stage production. We were outdrawing every theater in town. I had to vary my practice, so that it did not get monotonous, and I could not spend too much time talking to the boys because the people wanted action... Coaching in Indiana was never like this.[17]

At an exhibition game shortly before the team was to depart for Italy, the chairman of the Republic of China Olympic Committee presented Odle with two trophies on behalf of the ROC government, one noting the "everlasting friendship" between Americans and Chinese, and the other "To Mr. Odle Coach of the Chinese National Basketball Team... With distinguished guidance marching for victory."[18]

After a final exhibition game against an all-star team from the Philippines, the ROC squad was ready to travel to Rome. The chartered plane was required to make a series of stops including Hong Kong, Bangkok, and Calcutta before arriving in Rome. It quickly became apparent travel delays as well as international politics would plague the ROC athletes. A thorny question was whether ROC really represented all of China or just Taiwan. Because India and the Republic of China did not have diplomatic relations, the situation became tense for the Chinese when they arrived in Calcutta and were forced to endure an eighteen hour delay. Odle recalls how his athletes "were all herded into a quarantine area and told to wait." Odle was instructed to remain with the team. Before they left the plane, the players were told to leave their money. However, they decided to give all the money to Odle for safe keeping which needless to say made "Coach" rather uncomfortable.

These delays made the situation very difficult for the Chinese. Even though they had little sleep, as soon as they arrived in Italy they were obliged to play several games in the qualifying rounds. The ROC basketball squad was one of twenty-two teams to participate in the qualifying rounds

What Price Glory — 1958-1964

in Bologna, Italy to take place between August 13 and 22 competing for the four remaining slots. Twelve of the sixteen teams for the basketball tournament had qualified by July 5. Thus ROC was a long shot in obtaining a slot for the final rounds. An additional problem arose regarding under what name the ROC team should play. After much discussion, it was forced to agree to be identified as "Taiwan" and not China.

"Coach" felt the ROC squad's most important asset was speed when the players were fully rested. But this turned out not to be the case as a result of the long trip and the serious delay in Calcutta. On August 14 Spain defeated the Nationalist Chinese by a score of 83-55. This was a serious blow to ROC's chances. Then on August 17 Taiwan lost to the Czech team 86-67. But the *Manila Times* reported that "the Czechs had to call on every ounce of strength and every inch of height advantage to overcome the Chinese... Taiwan closed within five points midway in the second half before the Czechs steadied themselves."[19] The Chinese team lost three contests and won three, upsetting Austria by a lopsided score of 107-78. But this record was not good enough to obtain a berth for the final tournament of the sixteen top teams.[20] Nevertheless, the Chinese could take some pride in that they ranked fifth among the twelve non-qualifying teams, with a higher ranking than Austria, Thailand, Great Britain, Switzerland, Surinam, Australia, and the Sudan.

There were positive comments and sympathy for the Chinese squad. A Bologna newspaper noted the following:

> The team that received the greatest success and sympathy at the pre-Olympic tourney was that of Taiwan... The public supported them openly at each game, but it was not the spontaneous sympathy toward the weakest team; it was rather the result of an unconditional approval for fine play, their dynamic playing. This playing was inspiring and entertaining to all of the fans. The Chinese did not come to Bologna just to win, they came in humility to show that which they could demonstrate well and to learn from others. At the end all had to recognize that the game of basketball was bred for them. Some

of their more famous opponents discovered that they had much to learn from the Chinese team.[21]

Despite the disappointing record at the Olympics, the team was still heroized in Taiwan. Following the Olympics, Odle received numerous accolades for his work. Yi Kuo-jui, lieutentant general of the China Armed Forces and the head of the China National Basketball Association, wrote Odle a letter in which he stated:

> I wish to take this opportunity to thank you sincerely for the wonderful service you rendered to the China Basketball Team. Your entire effort in coaching has not only benefited the team but also contributed immensely in promoting modern basketball technique on the whole. Earnestly I hope that constant contact between us in the future be maintained.[22]

VV Experiences in the Early 1960s

VV continued to send basketball teams to East Asia. The itineraries generally were of a similar pattern – first Japan, followed by Hong Kong, Taiwan, and ending in the Philippines. During some years Korea, Singapore, Malaysia, Thailand, Vietnam, and Indonesia were also included. Since Odle was coaching the Republic of China Olympic team, leadership responsibilities in 1960 were in the hands of Norm Cook and Bud Schaeffer. Tine Hardeman and Schaeffer set up the itinerary in the Philippines and Norm Nelson, an Overseas Crusades missionary in Taiwan, made the plans there.[23]

The 1960 team consisted of Mel Peterson (Wheaton), Ray Ritsema (Hope College), John Van Dixhorn (Northwestern College), Tom Morgan (Greenville College), Willie Preston (Rice University) and two Taylor players, Tim Diller (he was on three teams—1960, 1962, 1963) and Ken Hudkins. Hardeman and Keith

What Price Glory — 1958-1964

Brown, members of previous VV teams who were serving in the Philippines, also joined the squad. According to the *Manila Times* these missionaries all played for the Philippine Air Lines Skymasters. The *Manila Times* noted Hardeman was the "star of the local PAL team."[24] All the players were over six feet except Hudkins and Morgan. Preston and Ritsema were the tallest at six-five.[25]

The team continued to do very well. They played a total of 80 games (38 in Taiwan, 4 in Hong Kong and 38 in the Philippines), winning 75, losing 4 (2 to the Philippine Olympic team; two to the Republic of China Olympic team), and one tie (the Republic of China Olympic team). The audience totaled some 200,000 people. In Taiwan every radio

1960 VV team

station carried the games and major newspapers included articles and photographs. Clearly the featured games were played against the Republic of China Olympic team coached by Odle. Also, the squad held 55 additional meetings, and about 2,000 enrolled in the Bible correspondence course.[26]

Following a successful series in Hong Kong, the VV team concluded its summer games in the Philippines between July 21 and 30. As in the past, long descriptive stories about the contests were published in numerous newspapers in the Philippines including the *Manila Times*. Its writers continued to refer to the VV players as "towering bible-preachers" from the United States, and frequently referred to them as Taylor University Trojans even though only Diller and Hudkins were Taylor students.[27] Its reporters noted

The VV team preaching the Gospel

that the Americans had a "decided edge in height and weight."[28] "Height and deadly outside shooting again formed the difference for the American Bible-preachers", noted the *Manila Times* on July 26 in an article describing a game in which the VV team "blasts" the Businessmen's AA selection, 102-71. "Height is Might" began a photo caption in the July 29, 1960 edition of the *Manila Times* describing "long-limbed" Willie Preston keeping the ball away from the YCO-PAL cagers in a contest in which VV defeated YCO-PAL 96-81. The Americans were described as "tall, heavy and exceptionally sharp" in a game in which VV "wallops" a M.I.C.A.A. combination team 103-79.

By far the most exciting games in Manila in July 1960 were the contests between VV and the Philippine Olympic team which was heading for the Rome Olympiad in August. The Filipinos saw the games as a way "to boost the... Olympic fund drive" and hopefully a morale booster for the team in light of the Taiwanese Olympic squad's two victories earlier in the summer. There were heightened expectations as the two teams squared off at Rizal Coliseum in two games on July 26 and 29. In the first match some 9000 fans assembled in Manila's arena. Many people were apprehensive wondering if their team could really subdue the Americans. During the first half of the contest, the VV players were in usual form, jumping out to an early 39 to 23 lead. But in the second half, the *Manila Times* reported the PI Olympians "drove 9,000 fans crazy with a blazing 44-point rally that paid off in victory in the last four minutes.... The Philippine Olympians battled up from a nightmarish first half... and slugged out a 67-62 morale-booster over the Venture for Victory cagers" reported the *Manila Times*.[29] The local reporter also noted that the VV team was "visibly fatigued, and their tempers worn by the Filipinos' rugged defense."[30] It was clear that the Filipinos were much more aggressive then they were in the early 1950s.

A rematch between VV and the Philippine Olympians took place three days later. "We're ready to settle the score," noted Coach Schaeffer.[31] A packed crowd of 11,000 witnessed the contest in Rizal Coliseum. Once again the Filipinos were behind during the first half. But in the third quarter they battled back. The *Manila Times* reporter described the second half. "The sweltering spectators kept up a steady roar as Yburan Ortiz, Cruz Ocampo, and [Edgardo] Roque limited the surprised Americans to four points for seven minutes. If they weren't stealing the ball, they were harrassing the Americans, spoiling their passes and shots, out jumping them right under their own basket."[32] The Filipinos' "fast passing attack... gained extra viciousness with Ortiz' deadliness."[33] The result was another stun-

1962 followup card

ning victory for the Philippine Olympians by a narrow margin of 75-72. This game was a reminder that VV no longer could count on continued victories. Coach Odle commented that the Philippine teams were decidedly rougher in their competitiveness than other East Asian teams.[34] This trend would continue to build throughout the early 1960s.

The year 1961 was somewhat unique in that only two college cagers —Ray Durham and Maurice Paul, both Taylor University students—were sent from the United States to join missionary athletes in East Asia.

In 1962 Odle was again suffering from back injuries and his place as coach was taken by Norm Cook. In that year two Taylor players—Diller and Dave Kastelein— were on the team. Kastelein was a football, basketball, and track star at Taylor. When he was inducted into the Taylor University Athletic Hall of Fame in 1973, the citation noted that he was all conference fullback in 1962-3, Indiana's top scorer in football in 1962, NAIA district all-American in 1963, and he set a new pole vault record in 1962. "A team leader and competitor he stood head and shoulder above his competitors." The photogenic Kastelein took a leading role in a film about Venture for

Dave Kastelein and Bud Schaeffer featured in the VV film

Victory produced in 1962 by Ken Anderson Studios of Warsaw, Indiana. Kastelein and Diller were joined by players from UCLA, Georgia Tech, Southern California University, Pasadena College, Oklahoma City University, and Huntington College (Alabama).

Diller grew up in Bluffton, Ohio, and was a basketball star in high school. An important influence in young Diller's life was Taylor University alumnus Paul

What Price Glory — 1958-1964

Steiner. At the time, Steiner was youth director in Diller's church. He brought the young star to a Taylor youth conference which resulted in Diller's application and acceptance to that college in 1958. He played basketball in his freshman year but it was not until his second year that he joined the varsity team. In his junior year he was selected to be on the VV team.

Diller recalls he had never been outside the United States and there was little orientation before the team left. But once in East Asia the missionaries gave the cagers much useful information about the local culture. Diller remembers the teams VV played were a full spectrum ranging from very tough professional teams to easy pick up type games. The team played at a leprosarium, at prisons, and at all sorts of schools. Huge numbers of people attended the games because people just loved basketball. Playing conditions varied widely from good conditions at Rizal Coliseum to night games in small towns where the players had to play under two lights each placed above the baskets which in turn attracted swarms of insects. Sometimes "the best thing to do was to shoot out the lights", recalls Diller. The basketball hoops varied in height from eight to ten feet. One of his vivid memories was that frequently the referees showed favoritism towards the home team. Diller added, "This is where you let your Christianity show... In the back of your mind was the thought that you were there as a witness."[35]

Tim Diller

The response of the people to the Gospel was "amazing". At half time the audience would listen attentively to the music and testimonies. The players were often joined by missionaries, one of whom would give a short sermon. It was always "well organized."

171

Singing at half time

Diller sang in a quartet which always made a hit with the crowd. Sometimes, admits Diller, there was "oppression" at half time. For example, there were occasions when the loudspeakers would mysteriously stop working.

A daunting challenge for the players was sleeping on concrete floors in villages and small towns. "It was not a comfortable environment." An additional challenge for the team was the meals which sometimes included cold eggs that had been cooked hours before we came and learning to eat them even though they were unpalatable. But the players also learned how people gave generously to the team. "The missionaries pulled out the last can of peaches for us." It was a character changing time for Diller and opened his mind to the possibility of becoming a missionary.[36]

In 1962 VV won 57 games and lost nine. Of these, VV beat the Japanese Asian Games national team

Ministering to the armed forces

What Price Glory — 1958-1964

twice and lost to them once. It won 3 and lost 3 to the Republic of China's national squad, lost a game to Taipei's Seven Tigers and lost 3 to the Philippine Asian Games team.[37] Schaeffer commented that VV suffered more injuries in 1962 than any other previous team. Despite this difficulty the cagers witnessed to about 200,000 people in Japan, Taiwan and the Philippines. A large number of people enrolled in the Bible course, over 20,000 in the Philippines alone.[38]

Diller preaching

As usual competition was particularly keen in the Philippines. The VV team arrived in Manila from Hong Kong in early July to begin a grueling schedule of twenty-four contests. Immediately after deplaning in Manila the squad played the Philippine Chinese Youth Selection, easily defeating them 90-53. According to Bill McKee, chief

Coach Odle speaking through an interpreter

173

of VV operations in the Philippines the Americans were suffering from "bum stomachs" during this point in the trip.[39]

The major contests that year featured the VV squad against the Philippine national team slated to go to the Asia Games to be held in early August in Jakarta, Indonesia. The Philippines was the defending Asia Games champion. The VV squad geared up for these three dramatic contests to be held in the 25,000 seat Araneta Coliseum in Quezon City. The *Manila Times* noted that "the Philippine Asian Games quintet goes through its first acid test... when it meets the Venture for Victory hoopsters, a crack crew of American collegians." Thousands of Filipinos were looking forward to "the attractive brand of basketball which V for V and Philippine teams have waged in the past."[40] A local sports reporter noted that six foot one inch Chris Appel, University of Southern California guard, was "the heart" of the VV game but another man to watch was Gary Cunningham, 6-5, from UCLA.[41] The same article also noted that "a fine performance by the local boys is particularly important from a psychological point of view considering the fact that the Japanese Asian Games team managed to get [defeat] the V for V five in one of three games they played in Tokyo last month."[42]

Excitement grew as the two teams squared off on July 10 before 20,000 exuberant spectators. The Philippine national team started out with "early jitters" but opened up a 45-36 lead at half time and tore the game wide open in the last two minutes with an outburst of blinding fastbreaks.

> They beat Don Odle's taller Bible-preachers in every department, particularly in the rebounds where they outjumped V for V by a staggering score of 36 to 14. The boys moved like wildcats in defense, outmaneuvering the Americans on every turn and holding them off to the fringes, and broke into the V for V's backcourt with impunity to strike from under as often as they did from outside.[43]

What Price Glory — 1958-1964

Exciting competition

Thirty-two year old Carlos Loyzaga who had played against VV teams since the early 1950s was the clear star for the Filipinos. A sports reporter commented VV's hero was Chris Appel, "a slick backcourt general."[44] It was a rough and tumble game. McKee complained about some of the calls of the referees, noting that "foul calls were not proportionate... Once the referees called 12 straight fouls against us and then I kept my eye on the 30-second area and there were times the local boys stayed there longer than they should. Those little things really killed us."[45] The sports writer for the *Manila Times* also commented on some poor calls. "Many snapping contacts by the locals were not called." But he added "better officiating would never have weakened the Filipinos' energetic display."[46] McKee of Philippine Crusades called the playing skill of the Filipinos "fabulous" and said "if they don't keep the Asian Games title, they ought to swim back [from Jakarta]. They were sharp in everything – their timing, shooting, passing, their defense." Coach Odle "praised the Filipinos' shooting but said his boys 'were off their usual form.'"[47]

Everyone was prepared for the second contest held on July 12 in which some 25,000 excited fans filled the Araneta Coliseum. The *Manila Times* noted that "thirsty for vengeance, the playing missionaries who have lost only thrice in 23 games promise to turn the tables on the Filipinos."[48] Tine Hardeman was quoted as saying, "It will be a different story. They [VV players] are in greater shape."[49] But despite a very close game, the Philippine Asian Games quintet once again defeated the VV cagers, this time by a very close score of 76-74. Many people thought the officiating tended to favor the Filipinos over the Americans, but Coach Odle would not comment on this assertion. The *Manila Times* sports reporter noted the following in his story:

> Odle praised the Filipinos saying 'they're undoubtedly the better team. We gave our best, and still we lost. There was simply nothing we could do against your marvelous team.[50]

Despite the disappointment among the VV players, they stoically went on to play 20 contests in various parts of the Philippines, winning each game, and looking forward to the final confrontation with the Philippine national team held July 30 in Quezon City. Ever the optimist, Hardeman commented to the *Manila Times* reporter, "Of course, the boys are a little tired after playing 20 games in two weeks... But I think they are really up. We ought to win this one." Due to recurring back injuries, Odle had returned to the United States and the coaching responsibilities were in Bud Schaeffer's hands. Before a crowd estimated at 20,000, the local heroes led by Carlos Loyzaga once again defeated the VV team. "Philippine cagers subdue Venture for Victory, 71-62" ran the banner headline in the *Manila Times*.[51]

The 1960 and 1962 summer experiences for VV clearly showed the local national teams could indeed effectively challenge and defeat them, and indeed this would continue during the next couple of years. Yet VV continued to be very successful in defeating local teams in East Asia. Following the July 30 game, VV headed to Taiwan for a three week series.[52]

The schedule for the 1963 season began in Korea followed by Hong Kong, Cambodia, Singapore, Indonesia, Philippines and Guam. The team members for that year were Tim Diller (then attending Fuller Seminary) and players from Anderson College, Grace College, University of Wyoming, Harvard University, Biola College and Springfield College in Massachusetts.[53]

What Price Glory — 1958-1964

They included Gene Augustine, Barrett Bates, Clyde Cook, Tim Diller, Al Eastland, Bob Hilts, Glen Kamerrer, and Gordon Merton.[54] A total of over 162,000 Asians witnessed 48 games, in which the VV team won 38 contests, lost 9, and tied one. Over 4000 people enrolled in Bible courses.[55] Fewer games were scheduled because greater emphasis was placed on competing in large stadiums in major cities rather than playing more informal games in the barrios. This decision carried a cost; personal one-on-one evangelism was difficult in the large stadiums. The team continued its half time ministry, but the after game interaction with the fans was made more difficult.[56]

Clyde Cook had just recently arrived in the Philippines where he was serving with Overseas Crusades as a missionary when he received a telegram from Dick Hillis saying that Bill Bradley, all American at Princeton University and a future United States Senator from New Jersey, at the last moment was instructed by his coach not to join the VV team for fear of injury. The telegram requested that Cook replace Bradley immedately. Cook responded by flying to Tokyo where he joined VV.

Cook recalls that there had been a quantum leap in the caliber of basketball competition between

Clyde Cook

1957, his last involvement with VV, and 1963. In all countries there was tougher competition, to a great extent because of the increased height of the players. In the first game in Korea "we found ourselves ten points down in the last period" but were able to "tie up the score. We wanted to go into overtime but the Koreans objected. We wanted to win, but the Koreans said, 'No, we'll end it at a tie.'"[57]

In Cambodia recalls Cook, the referees made questionable decisions. "Whenever we got close to them the referees would frequently call ten second violations against VV." The Americans found this hard to take and objected to these calls. "We were not a very good testimony. The Cambodian newspaper blasted us." It was particularly frustrating for the VV players because they were playing professional teams who billed themselves as amateurs.[58]

As was the case in the previous couple of years, some of the toughest competition came in the Philippines. Of the nine losses, three were there, the most for any single country. VV arrived in Manila on August 3. That same evening, the team, coached by Schaeffer, was scheduled to play Ysmael Steel, one of the three top teams of the M.I.C.A.A. League in Rizal Stadium. On August 5, the team played Crispa, and two days later, Yco Painters, two other top M.I.C.A.A. League teams. The *Manila Times* referred to these teams as "the Big Three of 'local hoopdom'" who all eagerly sought to defeat VV. Schaeffer was well known in Manila because he had starred on two Philippine teams, Seven-Up and Philippine Air Lines.

The *Manila Times* as usual was complimentary about the VV team. "A no-nonsense outfit with a tight schedule that could wear down a less spartan squad, the venturers are usually in peak form by the time they swing over to the Philippines where they say they enjoy the competition."[59] This compliment, however, placed increased pressure on the team. Unfortunately several of the VV players had experienced illness and fever just prior to their arrival in Manila which weakened their stamina.[60]

What Price Glory — 1958-1964

VV's winning record was shattered when it was defeated in quick succession by these top three M.I.C.A.A. teams. It was clear the Philippine players were fast whereas the Americans exhibited fatigue. In the first game, Ysmael Steel, the national and M.I.C.A.A. champions, "wore the tall American Bible preachers down with their fast, pressing game to pull away early in the second half, after a see-sawing first half ended at 46-all."[61] The final score was 89-76. After the game, Schaeffer graciously complemented the Ysmael team. On August 5, the Redmanizers of the Crispa team edged VV 95-92. *The Manila Times* noted: "Crispa fought back furiously in the last nine minutes to deal the visiting Venture for Victory cagers their second straight Philippine setback... Ironically it was [former] Venturer Gary Cunningham himself who engineered the Redmanizers' come-from-behind victory before a sparse crowd of almost 2,000."[62] Cunningham was a regular on the Crispa team. The Americans lost wind in the closing minutes. "Taller and heavier, the Americans dominated the rebounds three-fourths of the way, but they eventually lost steam in the closing minutes and were soon beaten to the rebounds by their smaller but faster rivals."[63]

The following day the *Manila Times'* sports page featured this headline: "Yco Painters blitz V for V cagers, 96-82". The sports writer noted that "Yco, keeping up with its rivals, ravaged the Venture for Victory cagers last night in a wild, bruising contest... It was the Venturer's third straight defeat... and boosted already fierce interest in Yco's MICAA title showdown Saturday with Ysmael Steel."[64] Carlos Loyzaga, VV's old nemesis, was again the Philippine hero. The *Manila Times* pointed out that although VV controlled the rebounds, "the blistering pace and Yco's harassing man to man forced them [VV] into hurried shots... Yco maintained a full fastbreaking velocity throughout and struck with terrorizing accuracy from all angles as they kept the ball out of the Venturers' longer reach with speedy passes and quick screens."[65]

Schaeffer attributed the defeats to the skill and excellence of play on the part of the Philippine teams.

Their timing was excellent and "their positioning in the rebounds the best in the Orient. Smooth is the word to describe the boys here." But he also noted that the heat and humidity in most countries the VV team visited wore down the players more than the hectic schedule. Finally Schaeffer praised the referees. "It is more like the refereeing we're used to in the States." He expressed his team's appreciation for the "finesse that your basketball players show in all respects. We enjoyed the three games very much, although we didn't play as well as we had hoped to."[66] The rest of the contests in the Philippines, however, went better for VV. The Americans swept games against other teams in Manila, Cebu, and Iloilo, winding up with a winning record in the Philippines.

The *Manila Herald* noted that the team would be leaving Manila on August 10, but that Gary Cunningham would remain behind in the Philippines to teach at the American School in Manila and continue to play for Crispa. Schaeffer would continue his mission work in Cebu and was joined by Clyde Cook and his wife.[67] The Cooks remained in the Philippines as Overseas Crusades missionaries until 1967. The VV experience helped Cook to determine that he wanted to work with Overseas Crusades. He saw their missionaries as "sharp, on the cutting edge, flexible. I wanted to be identified with that type of missionaries." During those years Cook and Schaeffer regularly flew to Manila to play on the Philippine Airlines team in tournaments. The news coverage was extensive. Since the Filipinos were avid newspaper readers, word spread quickly about the exploits of the VV team and the prowess of Cook and Schaeffer, resulting in greater visibility for the missionaries' endeavors.[68]

What Price Glory — 1958-1964

1964 – The End of an Era

It was apparent that in the early 1960s the VV teams continued to play well against second ranked squads, but competition had become much more intense against nationally renowned Asian teams. VV cagers were not faring well against these latter netmen in Japan, Korea, Taiwan, and particularly in the Philippines whose teams were considered the best in East Asia. In 1962 VV lost all its three games to the Philippine Asian Games quintet, and in 1963 they had an even worse record when they lost to the three M.I.C.A.A. teams – Ysmael, Crispa, and Yco – by fairly wide scores. This was certainly disappointing and frustrating to both VV's leaders and players. Odle wanted to turn around this string of defeats. He was determined to recruit and organize an extremely strong team for the summer of 1964. As a column in the *Manila Times* noted, "After the six thrashings its predecessors received here [in the Philippines] the last two years, organizers of the 1964 Venture for Victory aggregation saw to it that revenge would be sweet, if not complete."[69]

The 1964 VV team.

COACH ODLE'S FULL COURT PRESS

Don Odle was quoted as saying that the 1964 Venture for Victory team was the strongest he had organized since its inception in 1952.[70] He was determined to challenge successfully the vastly improved Asian teams. The team was described as "taller and more powerful than all previous V-V outfits" including eight six-footers.[71] The 1964 team consisted of two players each from Kansas State University (Dave Nelson, Jeff Simons), and the University of Georgia (Jerry Waller, Mack Crenshaw), as well as one each from Vanderbilt University (Clyde Lee – he was 6-9, the tallest on the team), Northwest Nazarene College (Gary Locke), the University of Kentucky (Terry Mobley), the University of Kansas (Nolen Ellison), and Taylor University (Bob Stewart). Odle's son Dave, a senior in high school, also was a member of the team. Tine Hardeman joined the team as did Chris Appel who took Terry Mobley's position as a guard after he broke his knee cap in a game in Hong Kong and was forced to return to the United States. The *Manila Times* referred to the team's five leading players as the "Stratospheric five."[72]

During part of 1962 and in 1963, Bud Schaeffer had coached the team, but in 1964 Odle decided again to take on this responsibility. It was his desire to lead the team to a resounding success on the basketball court in all the countries the squad was to visit – Japan, South Korea, the Republic of China, and finally the Philippines. During the two previous years the team had a grueling schedule, and when the players finally arrived in the Philippines to play highly competitive squads, they appeared exhausted and frequently ill. Odle was determined to avoid this in 1964 by making sure his cagers were rested and in peak form to compete against the Philippine national team in late August.

In many ways 1964 was one of the most successful summers for the VV cagers in terms of victories on the court. But frequently when the pinnacle of success is reached, individuals and organizations are reminded of the need for a reappraisal of aspirations or goals,

What Price Glory — 1958-1964

and perhaps to consider aiming in a new direction. This was the situation Odle found himself in in 1964. He was about to take on added responsibilities at Taylor as assistant to the president in charge of public relations. He was also experiencing "burn out" with respect to organizing and publicizing the VV program. The summer of 1964 was a time of phenomenal success for VV, but it was also a painful disappointing season. A situation not necessarily conducive to effective evangelization was about to reach a climax.

The summer began somewhat shakily when the VV squad lost a contest in Tokyo to the Japanese national team by a score of 75-70 in overtime. It was reported that VV was "crippled by international rules."[73] But the team roared back, defeating the same Japanese squad on five succeeding engagements, winning one contest by as much as 40 points.[74] In fact the earlier loss to the Japanese national team proved to be the only one the cagers suffered that summer in Korea, Taiwan and Hong Kong. In both Korea and Taiwan, VV swept all the games with the Korean and Nationalist Chinese Olympians. In the final game in Hong Kong, VV crushed the Hong Kong All-Stars by a lopsided score of 88-53. When the team arrived in the Philippines on August 20, it had amassed an astound-

1964

183

ing record of 34 wins, one loss. The only other setback was guard Terry Mobley's knee injury sustained in Hong Kong during the previous week. Chris Appel who had played on the 1962 VV team and who had helped train the Cambodian national team during the last two years quickly was assigned to Mobley's position.[75]

Keith Brown of Philippine Crusades had helped to organize the Philippine part of VV's schedule with the Basketball Association of the Philippines. VV was scheduled to be in the Philippines from August 20 to the end of the month. Games were scheduled against several teams including a "top-flight" local team in Olongapo, Zambales on August 24, but the big exhibition games were with the Philippine Olympic five (RP) at the Rizal Coliseum on August 22, 26, and 29 with a possible fourth game to be played in Baguio, north of Manila. The RP team saw these contests as a good "tuneup" to the Yokohama elimination rounds coming up to qualify for the Tokyo Olympics in September.[76] "The Philippine team's mettle for the Yokohama eliminations will undergo its first formal test tonight (August 22) against the highly-touted Venture for Victory quintet at the Rizal Coliseum", trumpeted the *Manila Times*.[77] "The match... will mark the first outing of the national quintet since it was formed two weeks ago." Despite rainy weather, some 9,000 ardent fans were in their seats in the Coliseum by 6:00 PM for the beginning of the well-publicized contest. By intermission the VV team was ahead 44-39. The lead scorer for VV was Jerry Waller who eventually netted 31 points in the game. The second half continued to be a hard-fought contest. Ultimately it resulted in a VV victory.

The headlines the next day in the *Manila Sunday Times* read: "V-V cagers rip RP team, 84-72." The article noted: "The Venture for Victory quintet, a pack of fast, sharp-shooting behemoths, trampled the Philippine Olympic five... Height, speed and a scoring sock never before displayed by a V for V outfit here, gave the visiting Bible-preachers the lopsided triumph before 9,000 fans..."[78] It was reported the VV dribblers outclassed the RP cagers in all departments includ-

What Price Glory — 1958-1964

ing "fastbacks" which usually was conceded to the Filipinos. The Americans cashed in on height and "razor-sharp shooting" and were able to fend off a "vicious" rally on the part of the RP team. It was described as a "bruising match." Odle gave high praise to Renato Reyes on the Philippine team. The article observed Reyes attacked "the massive VV defense with a bravado that bordered on the insolent."[79] The energetic Coach Valentine "Tito" Eduque stated that his team "ran out of gas in the stretch, victims of their own speed, but that's what we're working on right now. Stamina."[80] The *Manila Times* concluded that "the game proved that the local Olympians have still a lot to work on if the Philippines must hurdle the Yokohama eliminations to qualify for the tournament proper in the Tokyo Olympics."[81] It was a sweet victory for VV after its string of defeats against leading Philippine teams during the two previous years.

Emotions were at fever pitch among the fans and players in Rizal Coliseum for the evening rematch on August 26. A reporter described the contest as a "hard, aggressive game" replete with fiery exchanges and with tempers running high. The VV team held the lead throughout most of the game. Then the Filipinos poured it on, outscoring VV 16-7 "in the last six minutes of the wildly exciting contest."[82] The article noted: "The Philippine Olympians, fighting like wildcats all the way, overhauled an 11-point Venture for Victory lead in the last quarter and held the stratospheric Americans to a spine tingling 80-all deadlock... The stalemate went unresolved over the protests of the Americans, as well as the 10,000 spectators who had been thrown into a frenzy by the Filipinos' hard, aggressive game."[83] It was reported that one VV player exclaimed, "We didn't travel this far only to play a tie."[84]

Coach Odle clearly was upset by the excessive roughness of the game, particularly on the part of the Philippine team. Three of his players-Clyde Lee, Nolen Ellison, and Jerry Waller – were injured and were forced get medical attention from an American doctor. The following day Odle announced that VV had decided to withdraw from the third game against the Philippine Nationals due to injuries, and immediately to send home these three players as well as Jeff Simmons and Dave Nelson who claimed they needed to leave in order to get to college classes. Calling off the last game was "my best judgment", Odle told reporters. "I must put the health of the boys first."[85] This resulted in a strong reaction from Senator Ambrosio Padilla, president of the Basketball Association of the Philippines. He said Odle's decision to send home the five players was "unilateral." He added that "the least you [Odle] could have done was get in touch with us" before making the announcement. "The picture you are trying to make out is that we are the criminals and you are the angels." Then he bluntly stated, "In my opinion, this will be the last time you will be invited here."[86]

The following day, the *Manila Times* carried a column by sports writer Antonio Siddayan entitled "This one smells." It was a rebuke to both teams, but particularly to VV. The columnist touched upon a variety of issues involving basketball competition in the Philippines. One theme that was repeated in the press throughout the years was the height and weight of the American players which was a great advantage to them over their Asian opponents. The latter then had to rely on speed and scrapiness. The column quoted from Dionislo Calvo, secretary of the Basketball Association of the Philippines. "Our biggest boys bounce off like cardboard boxes when hit by those bigger guys." So it is "absolutely necessary for the little men to fight like wildcats." The sports writer then noted,

> If the Filipinos were at fault in overdoing their underground warfare once too often, so were the playing padres guilty in another, more serious degree. Deciding on the cancellation all by themselves and shutting the door to any remedy by sending home five players, not just three who were injured, was a blur on the American image of fair play – a slight that outrages any right thinking Filipino who feels that the men who run the local association... are not above reason and understanding.

What Price Glory — 1958-1964

> Damning Clyde Lee's injury as a lowly crime inten-
> tionally inflicted by a punch... and then using this as
> a key to the cancellation smacked of typical American
> highhandedness.[87]

The column also questioned why Odle referred the
injured players to an American doctor rather than
someone from the Philippine medical profession. The
writer went on to wonder why "Coach" allowed two
players to leave "on the flimsy excuse that they had to
catch the start of classes on Monday."

One can argue that the Filipinos were oversensi-
tive on some points, but the American decision had
not taken into account a number of sensibilities. The
column continued with the following admonition:

> Odle's boys could have played just one more game,
> this being the last of the tour, and they still would not
> have lost face.... They would have looked nobler fight-
> ing... with the three crippled mainstays on the bench.
> Silently and deeply admired for steadfastly refusing to
> strike back under stress of the kind that would have
> broken lesser men, they would have evoked compassion
> in the gallery, which is essentially Christian after all.

Odle's position was that the game was cancelled
because conditions were "unsafe, unhealthy and we
knew it would be very unwise to try to play a game
under such explosive conditions... I was responsible
for the health and safety of all these young men...
I cancelled the basketball game due to injuries, illness, fatigue and some very unsafe conditions. I felt
it was unwise and dangerous to subject these athletes
to a game that could have devastating consequences."
Odle stated that the Filipinos "got tired of our winning
and turned to some very unsafe, unsportsmanlike,
and unethical practices in an effort to win. But there
was more to it than that. There were some 'Yankee Go
Home' signs posted before we arrived concerning some
other groups." Odle also noted that there were anti-
Protestant feelings in strongly Catholic Philippines.

Odle added that for fourteen years he had worked with the Philippine Basketball Committee and never had any problems until 1964.[88]

This incident was a deep embarrassment to all concerned. Odle returned with the team to the United States, tired and upset. There was much fence mending that needed to be done. Odle noted that eventually good relations were again reestablished.[89] Contact was maintained with the various Philippine teams despite the fact that in 1965 the Philippines was not included in the VV itinerary. Tine Hardeman, for example, continued to play for the Philippine Air Lines squad. But VV competition with the top national teams in large stadiums such as Rizal Coliseum in Manila and sizeable press coverage would no longer continue. Other American teams would move into that spotlight.

In the years following 1964 the VV program turned to competition with local teams rather than national ones. This change marked a return to a greater emphasis on the evangelistic dimension which to an extent had been lost in some games during the later years. The year 1964 was the last one in which Odle coached the team. Although he continued as Director of VV for two more years, leadership was passing to Bud Schaeffer. The organizational structure of Overseas Crusades also changed; a new division was created known as Sports Ambassadors. The responsibility for recruiting and fielding sports teams came under this division. In some parts of the world, especially in the Philippines and Taiwan where Venture for Victory was well known, the team continued to play under this rubric. Implementing this new format enabled OC's sports evangelistic ministry to expand gaining influence world wide.

What Price Glory — 1958-1964

   Chapter Seven

THE POWER OF MANY

Though 1964 can be seen as signaling the end of an era, it is by no means the end of Taylor University's involvement in the rapidly expanding phenomenon of sports evangelism nor was it the end of Don Odle's influence. From 1964 to the end of the twentieth century, Taylor's presence continued to be felt in several ways. First, the leadership of Sports Ambassadors/Venture for Victory (SA/VV) continued to follow the trail blazed by Odle in the 1950s and 1960s as his mantle fell first to Bud Schaeffer (1967-72) and then to Jack King (1973-79), both long time participants in this organization. Secondly, many of Taylor's star athletes were encouraged to participate on various SA/VV teams after 1964. Thirdly, Taylor coaches created innovative sports programs which were directly inspired by Odle's earlier VV model.

191

COACH ODLE'S FULL COURT PRESS

Bob Davenport's Wandering Wheels and Jack King's Friendship Sports are two significant programs with a clear sports evangelistic focus. Fourthly, through the expansion of the summer basketball camp located at Taylor University Coach Odle's impact on sports evangelism continued.

The Schaeffer Years – 1967-1972

In 1967 the leadership of SA/VV passed to Bud Schaeffer. One of the innovations which developed under his leadership was the creation of Crusader teams composed of career missionaries who played basketball throughout the year. During the first five months of 1967, the Crusader missionary team in the Philippines played 105 games, and as a result of those contests some 40,000 Filipinos signed up for the Bible correspondence course. Another innovation which

Bud Schaeffer

began during this time was the introduction of other sports to the SA/VV program. During the summer of 1967, two Wheaton College coaches took a track team to Mexico to hold clinics, participate in meets, and engage in evangelistic services. Additional opportunities opened up when the government in Taiwan invited Taylor University physical education instructor and baseball coach and former VV star, Jack King along with Jack Augustine (Taylor alumnus–class of 1955) of Barrington College to coach its Air Force baseball and basketball teams during the summer of 1967.[1]

While these innovations expanded the scope of SA/VV, the traditional summer basketball tours continued to be the main part of the total program. There were two VV basketball teams in 1968. Although they played before tens of thousands of people, literally millions more heard and watched the games and testimonies as a result of radio and television coverage. In Korea, for example, while 10,000 people attended one particularly competitive game, an estimated fifteen million people were tuned in via television and radio resulting in thousands signing up for the Bible correspondence course. While one team toured Japan, Korea, Taiwan, Hong Kong, and the Philippines winning 37 of its 50 contests, the second basketball squad journeyed to the South Pacific (Hawaii, Samoa, Fiji, New Zealand, Australia, New Caledonia), winning 33 games and losing 3 before smaller but enthusiastic audiences.[2]

The summer of 1969 broke new ground when SA/VV sent its first baseball team led by Taylor University coach Jack King to the Philippines, South Korea and Taiwan. King reported that over 60,000 people attended the team's first 16 games in East Asia.[3] The connection with the Republic of China military basketball teams was continued when Don Callan, Taylor alumnus, former VV player and coach at Cedarville College, went to Taiwan for a month. He then proceeded to Adelaide, Australia to assist with basketball teams and evangelism.[4] There was also a VV basketball team sent to South America.

COACH ODLE'S FULL COURT PRESS

Four basketball teams went to East Asia as well as Latin America during the summer of 1970, one of which was a women's team to Mexico. On the latter squad was Taylor athlete Judy Ruppert, and Bea Gorton, women's basketball coach at Wheaton College. In the late 1970s and early 1980s Gorton was professor of physical education and the women's basketball coach at Taylor. Also in 1970 a men's basketball squad coached by Paul Neuman who had played on the 1958 and 1959 VV teams journeyed to Latin America. He was a former All American basketball star from Stanford University, and played professional basketball in the National Basketball Association (NBA) for six years with the Philadelphia 76er's and the San Francisco Warriors. Another men's basketball squad went to East Asia headed by Norm Cook.

TU Coaches Carry on the VV Tradition

Two Taylor University baseball coaches, Jack King and Larry Winterholter, were destined to provide the link between the Taylor athletic department and SA/VV during the seventies and beyond.

King was born on a farm in Alexandria, Indiana, and in high school played baseball, football, and basketball.[5] After high school he was recruited by the Philadelphia Phillies. While playing with this major league team, he became a committed Christian. King played professional baseball for two years, and then entered Taylor University as a student in 1955. He was already married to Janet McCarthy and he recalls that he had several links with Taylor. His high school coach had played against Odle in the semi-professional league in Muncie in the late 1930s, and had brought King to see a Taylor basketball game in 1951. Another link was Ken Stark, a VV player on both the 1955 and 1956 teams who had given a talk about his VV experiences in King's Alexandria church.

The Power of Many

Jack King

When King and his wife began as students at Taylor in 1955, they thought they would be missionaries, and they took courses designed to lead them to that goal. But at the end of their freshman year, it was apparent to both of them that they were not missionary material. King started playing basketball at Taylor thanks to a rule change that allowed those who had been in professional ball to play in college sports. At the end of his junior year King joined the VV team.[6]

Following graduation from Taylor in 1959, King taught and coached two years in Elkhart, Indiana. Odle encouraged him to take the position of physical education instructor and baseball coach at Taylor in 1961. For the next decade King remained in that position. During his years of coaching King led Taylor's baseball team to five conference championships and a fourth place national ranking in 1969. He was invited to go to Taiwan as a coach/advisor to its air force baseball team in 1968. While in Taiwan a baseball team came from the Philippines to play in international competition. The coach was an evangelical, and asked King if he could bring a baseball team to the Philippines. In 1969 King took the first Sports Ambassadors baseball team including three Taylor athletes – Dennis Ladd, Ken O'Brien and Dave Tickner as well as Taylor alumnus Wayne (Tony) Ladd (class of 1964) - to East Asia.

Larry Winterholter grew up in the small town of Lancaster in Huntington County, Indiana. The town was so small that Odle used to say "Lancaster... is the only town in the state with the city limit signs on one post."[7] Winterholter was an outstanding basketball, baseball and track star during his high school years, motivating Odle to recruit him in 1960 to play basketball at Taylor. However, Winterholter proved to be more successful as a baseball star, and during his last three

195

years, he played under the coaching of Jack King.

After receiving his Taylor diploma in 1964, Winter-holter went on to graduate school at Illinois State University in Normal where he earned an M.S. degree in physical education. He then took a job at Malone College as baseball coach. He remained at Malone until the 1968-69 school year when he returned to Illinois State University as the assistant baseball coach while pursuing additional graduate studies.

While Winterholter was coaching at Illinois, Coach King contacted him to see if he had any players who would be interested in going on the tour to Latin America. Even though Winterholter did not have anyone to send, his own interest in being a part of an SA/VV experience was piqued and he asked if King could use him as an assistant coach. Although Winterholter had never been involved in a sports evan-gelism trip, King answered in the affirmative. Taylor's Dave Tickner who had played on the 1969 baseball team also was a part of this squad.

Honduras and Panama were the first two stops on the itinerary. Winterholter recalls that because there was a mix up concerning the arrival dates no teams were ready to play them causing some conster-nation for all involved. In Ecuador the audiences were not large which was disappointing for Winterholter. However, in Colombia and Venezuela the crowds were impressive giving the coaches and players a sense of exhilaration. In a stadium in Venezuela some 15,000 people turned out for the game. In Caracas, immedi-ately after the team deplaned late in the evening they were hustled through customs and taken to a sta-dium with the game commencing at 11:00 p.m. In the Dominican Republic, the final stop on the tour, the political situation was volatile, and for several days the team was not allowed to leave the hotel. Finally, they were able to play under the constant surveil-lance of armed guards patrolling the top of the dug-outs. For Winterholter, the high point of the trip was the personal relationships that developed, first between the teams and secondly between VV and the local people. He was shocked and deeply moved by a visit to an Ecuadorian barrio where he saw abject poverty and lack of basic sanitation.[8] This experience opened his mind to the opportunities inherent in sports evangelism.

Larry Winterholter

The basic evangelistic model established by Odle in the 1950s continued to be the pattern with modifications to better fit the structure of baseball games. If the team played a single game, there would be a ten minute presentation of songs and testimonies prior to the contest. If they were playing a double header, the evangelistic presentation was given between the games. A printed program containing a coupon to be filled out for those interested in signing up for a Bible correspondence course or being contacted by a local pastor or missionary was distributed to the fans. At the conclusion of the game the team stayed and visited with the players and coaches from the opposite squad. Meanwhile the coupons were collected from the stands and turned over to the missionaries for follow-up work. It was difficult for the players to make a direct contact with the spectators because the baseball field was frequently separated from the stands by a high fence.[9]

In retrospect, sports evangelism was not as effective with baseball games as in the more intimate setting of a basketball court. Nevertheless, the two major objectives of the tour — to present the Gospel and to build good will — were met. In addition to the pre-game testimonies, an important way in which these objectives were accomplished was having the players attend and participate in various Sunday local church services. As was the case with earlier VV basketball teams the two chief qualifications for participating on the SA/VV baseball team were to be a good athlete and to be able to verbalize a positive Christian witness. Not only was evangelism a key goal for the team, but also it was a conscious objective to help the players to grow spiritually.

Winterholter was profoundly impressed by both Don Odle and Jack King who constantly seized opportunities to share their faith with others and to pray for their team players. Although Winterholter recalled the team's schedule was grueling and he frequently became exhausted, this experience changed his life in a couple of meaningful ways. For the first time he found himself able to follow Odle and King's example to share the Christian message. In addition, his appreciation for different people and cultures was greatly enhanced.[10]

Two years after this second baseball tour Jack and Janet King decided to make a career change. They applied to Overseas Crusades and were accepted as missionaries. King's resignation from Taylor opened the way for Winterholter to return to his alma mater as baseball coach, a position he was to hold through the 2000-01 season.

During the first year the Kings were a part of Overseas Crusades they were assigned to spend a year at Multnomah School of the Bible in Oregon. King's passion for sports evangelism was unabated and he immediately set to work organizing a basketball team to go to British Columbia. This initiative paid off and for the next twenty years Multnomah sent teams to this Canadian province.

Following the year of training King became director of Sports Ambassadors and rapidly expanded the program, sending teams to various parts of the world. A number of fundamental changes were introduced. More summer teams were sent abroad and additional sports were added such as soccer. Women's teams became a regular occurrence. Latin America vied with East Asia as a venue for Sports Ambassadors activity while Africa, India and Mainland China were added to the growing list of opportunities. It was increasingly necessary to accommodate participants' desires to spend part of the summer working. New airline ticketing restrictions impinged on scheduling extended trips. As a result, SA/VV strategy was modified. There were more shorter trip opportunities available to college athletes who were drawn by the growing sports evangelistic ministry.

Gary Friesen represents a later group of Taylor University athletes who became involved with overseas sports evangelism. He was born in Japan in 1953; his parents were missionaries with Far Eastern Gospel Crusades (now Send, International). He attended the Alliance Academy for missionary children in Tokyo and graduated in 1971. He came to Taylor primarily because he "wanted to blaze his own trail".[11] Since he had played basketball in high school, Friesen tried out and was selected to play on the Taylor varsity team as a freshman and continued to play for the duration of his undergraduate years. He was a very gifted athlete. He lettered four

Gary Friesen

years in basketball and track, appeared in 108 basketball games for Taylor which established a new school record, set the school's shooting percentage record of 63.2%, won numerous state and national awards, and in both 1974 and 1975 he received the University's Gates-Howard Award.

Having grown up in East Asia, Friesen was familiar with the SA/VV program. In 1975, during his senior year at Taylor, he contacted Jack King who at that time was the director of Sports Ambassadors, expressing his interest in joining a team. Friesen was selected to be a member of the basketball squad which went to West Africa in that year. The 1975 team spent a week of orientation at The King's College in New York where they trained with their coach, Paul Neuman. The team spent one month in Africa, visiting Senegal, Nigeria, Liberia, and the Central African Republic. Africa presented a unique challenge because basketball was still in its infancy. Twenty-eight games were played against several highly-rated teams including Senegal's national netmen. In the Central African Republic the Americans competed against the four top club teams on consecutive nights, handily defeating them in the first three contests. But on the fourth night the Africans pooled their strongest players into one team, and "they didn't let us win that game!"[12] The summer's final record for the VV team was 24 wins and 4 losses.

The 1975 trip to Africa marked the beginning of Friesen's extended involvement with Sports Ambassadors and OC, its sponsoring missionary organization. The following year, he again was selected to play on a team headed for the Philippines coached by Tine Hardeman. The itinerary followed the approach developed after 1964 by competing against local provincial and university teams outside of Manila. Generally the games were played outdoors and keen fan interest continued with crowds averaging 2,000 per game.[13]

The year 1976 marked the 25th anniversary of the beginning of the VV/Sports Ambassadors Program. By that time more than 700 Christian athletes and coaches had played and preached in more than 60 countries through SA/VV men's basketball, baseball, soccer, track and field, and women's basketball teams. In that year eight basketball and baseball squads were sent to Latin America and East Asia involving 116 athletes. These trips generally were six to seven weeks in duration. Doug Winebrenner, a Taylor University senior physical education major, was on the basketball team to South America. There was a special SA alumni team to Taiwan and Hong Kong. In addition, Robin Cook, Schaeffer's son-in-law, conducted 313 basketball clinics in Papua New Guinea and Australia. It was reported that over 417,000 people attended the games and clinics. Of that number 36,500 participated in the Bible correspondence course and some 1,000 made decisions for Christ.[14]

The Power of Many

Gary Friesen ministering

Friesen did not join Sports Ambassadors in 1977, a year when five basketball teams and one baseball team were sent to Latin America and East Asia from mid-June to the end of July. But in 1978 he returned to West Africa as a "player-coach" with Robin Cook.[15] Sports Ambassadors also sent out one soccer, two baseball and seven basketball teams to a total of thirty countries with over 515,000 people in attendance. Some 138 athletes were involved. In Taiwan one of the basketball games was shown on national television where an estimated ten million people watched the game and heard the half time Gospel presentation.[16]

The summer of 1980 was a particularly eventful time for Friesen. He met his future wife, Janet Holsinger, daughter of Chuck and Betty Holsinger, and he participated in two basketball trips with SA/VV teams to the Philippines and to Mainland China. In the Philippines they competed against university teams in the Manila area. Phil Price, a Taylor alumnus (1978) who had played basketball with Friesen while they were in college was a member of the team. Friesen had not been scheduled to go to China, but when another player had to withdraw he was called and asked to join the squad. Friesen returned to China in 1982 on another SA/VV team. It was discovered that the level of basketball had greatly improved. The national teams they met on this trip had very tall players averaging 7' or more. SA/VV played ten games winning six and losing four, three of them in Beijing where they played national squads.[17]

Friesen had been teaching math at Eastbrook High School in Upland, Indiana, but in 1984 he resigned from this position. He and Janet were accepted by OC, and during the summer they interned with the mission in San Jose, California. In September, they were in the Philippines where Friesen taught math and coached the junior varsity basketball team at Faith Academy in Manila where he remained until 1996. During the time the Friesens were in the Philippines, he continued to play on SA/VV teams through the summer of 1992.

Jack King and Don Odle

Meanwhile Jack King resigned from the directorship of Sports Ambassadors at the end of 1979 in order to join Campus Crusade and its Athletes in Action branch. He remained with this organization until 1987 when he returned to Taylor to serve in the Office of Development. Winterholter recalls that in the 1980s the interest in SA/VV had abated at Taylor. However, King's return reinvigorated campus interest in overseas sports evangelism.

In 1990 Jack King, his wife Jan and son Jim created a new sports evangelism organization which they christened Friendship Sports. This organization continued to utilize many of the evangelistic strategies developed by Odle and the early VV teams while adding unique approaches to ministry. The basic aim of Friendship Sports is to impact a specific country with the Gospel. In order to accomplish this aim, King believes it is necessary for the same teams to return repeatedly, focusing their energies on a limited area and concentrating on building relationships with the indigenous people.

FRIENDSHIP SPORTS INTERNATIONAL

**GIRA AMISTOSA DE VOLIBOL
7-15 DE AGOSTO 1993
TEGUCIGALPA, HONDURAS**

Taylor University athletic teams have become involved in King's organization. The first Friendship Sports team was the Taylor women's volleyball squad coached by Karen Trout sent to the Dominican Republic. The Taylor baseball team coached by Winterholter has gone to Honduras in 1995, 1998 and 2001. Coach Don Taylor's men's tennis teams have also journeyed to Honduras where they participate in matches and conduct clinics with people from various economic strata. During most of the 1990s Honduras has been designated by Friendship Sports as the target country due in part to connections established by recent Taylor graduates, Scott and Mimi Barahona Crook. Friesen, who is now on the staff at Taylor University, has led Friendship Sports teams to Honduras.

Friesen believes that the overall impact of SA/VV and Friendship Sports is enormous. First, the effect on the young people who make up the teams is profound. It gives them the opportunity to see a world in need and to discover opportunities for ministry and service beyond the United States. Secondly, the people of the countries visited have been greatly impacted. "Hundreds of thousands have heard the

Gospel through these teams." Although it is impossible to measure precisely the number of converts, thousands of decision cards have been filled out and many Bible study correspondence courses completed.[18]

New Approaches to Sports Evangelism

Odle continued to be the basketball coach at Taylor during the 1970s. Although he ceased to be actively involved in recruiting and directing VV teams, it remained a cause close to Coach Odle's heart. He often talked about VV to his basketball players particularly in the weekly Bible studies that were held in his home. However, "Coach" understood that sports evangelism was not limited to short term missionary experiences abroad. He was equally aware of the opportunities on his own doorstep. At the same time that he was involved in creating Venture for Victory he was also actively expanding the summer basketball camp, a program developed in 1957 which through the years has attracted over 60,000 "aspiring young double-dribblers".[19]

In his unpublished *Taylor Made* Odle described how the idea of this successful program began. In 1956 Marion Crawley, famed Indiana high school basketball coach and an inductee of the Indiana Basketball Hall of Fame, invited Odle to be one of his speakers at an annual coaching clinic with over 500 coaches in attendance.[20] On this occasion the coaches were interested to learn about a Taylor University program called "The

Demonstrating basketball skills

Kampus Kids". In Odle's basketball class, students taught five and six year old boys various fundamentals of the game. After hearing Odle's presentation, Crawley suggested that a meeting be held to discuss how a summer basketball camp might be organized where fundamentals of the sport could be taught to young boys. At a meeting with Taylor Uni-versity officials, Odle and Crawley presented a proposal to establish a basketball camp during the summer of 1957, the first of its kind in the United States. The proposal was accepted. Newspapers and magazines wrote articles about the camp and coaches from many parts of the country came to observe the "experiment." Boys from both elementary and junior high school levels were accepted. A girl's activities camp paralleled the boy's basketball camp. The young women participated in cheerleading, baton twirling, gymnastics, horseback riding, crafts, swimming and tennis. When girl's basketball was introduced into the schools, the activities camp was transformed into a basketball camp.

Through the years Odle has attracted a number of sports heroes to participate in the summer basketball camps. They have included such renowned figures as Hallie Bryant of the Harlem Globe Trotters, Carl Erskine of the Brooklyn Dodgers, Bobby Richardson of the New York Yankees, Cazzie Russell from the NBA, Dick and Tom Van Arsdale of the Phoenix Suns and the New York Knicks, and Branch McCracken, Indiana University basketball coach. As a result of the wide impact of the basketball camp in the Midwest, Odle's name has become synonymous with Taylor University in the minds

Hallie Bryant and a young camper

of many people.

Odle retired as Taylor's head basketball coach in 1979 but he remained actively involved in the University's development department. Ever since his first trip with the VV team in 1952, his dream was to establish an evangelistic outreach in the People's Republic of China. The dream began to unfold in 1978 when he joined a tour and visited Canton, Shanghai and Beijing. As a result of this tour a young student from Shanghai named Gu Yue Xuan (Pamela Gu) was able to study at Taylor University under the Odles' sponsorship. In 1980 Odle was given the opportunity to direct an SA/VV basketball team trip to China to play seven exhibition games. The team was coached by Paul Neuman, and they landed in Hong Kong on August 5 beginning a week of practicing, playing and ministering. The squad won six contests, losing one in Shanghai where the American cagers played before a capacity crowd of 18,000. Although the team did not engage in the halftime evangelistic ministry because they were only the second sports team to play in China and they did not want to jeopordize further opportunities for such exchanges, they sang several songs including *Amazing Grace* and *How Great Thou Art.* After the eleven days in China they returned to Hong

Singing in a Shanghai stadium

The Power of Many

Kong where Odle was able to reestablish contact with Kuang Ko-yang (Billy Hwang) who had played basketball at Taylor in 1960-61.[21]

In addition to the China tour, Sports Ambassadors sponsored six other men's basketball teams to East Asia, South Asia, and Latin America in 1980. Also a women's basketball squad went to Latin America, a men's soccer team to Central America and the West Indies, and a men's basketball team to Latin America. The 119 athletes played and preached before a total of 338,000 people.

Wandering Wheels

It is clear that Odle's Venture for Victory made a strong impression on Taylor football coach Bob Davenport as he conceived and developed another Taylor University ground breaking sports evangelism organization, Wandering Wheels. Davenport was impressed by the stories of the early days of VV which demonstrated "a really gutsy vision." Odle's example inspired Davenport to believe in his own ability to do something significant and to wed athletics with the concept of Christian outreach.[22]

Wandering Wheels is a bicycle program officially incorporated in 1968 though the concept goes back to 1964. The founding spirit of Wheels was football All-American fullback Bob Davenport. He was born in Kansas but raised in southern California in a troubled home environment. He played football for UCLA in the early 1950s, setting numerous records and earning many accolades including Rookie of the Year, two years as all-American, Rose Bowl star, most valuable player and

Bob Davenport

207

leading scorer on UCLA's 1954 championship team.[23] While at UCLA Davenport came in contact with Bill Bright, a businessman who was active with the highly visible Hollywood Presbyterian Church. Bright had the vision of evangelizing the UCLA campus, especially the fraternity and sorority houses and beginning a program of Bible studies. He saw the need to go after "the campus stars", especially the athletes. Davenport was one of these leaders. As a result of these Bible studies, eight of the starting eleven 1954 UCLA football team members including Davenport had become believers. Bright took these young men to various meetings and encouraged them to give their testimonies. When Davenport turned professional he chose the Blue Bombers of Winnipeg, Manitoba over other teams who were anxious to acquire him. The major reason was Davenport's objection to play on Sundays; Canadian teams honored the Sabbath.[24]

Davenport first came into contact with Don Odle at a meeting in 1957 where "Coach" was the speaker. The subject of Odle's talk was the Venture for Victory program in East Asia. He showed slides and talked about issues confronting China. The main purpose of Odle's presentation was to publicize the VV program and to raise financial support. "I was mesmerized," recalled Davenport.[25] Odle was equally impressed by Davenport's athletic achievements. Davenport was "in transition" and Odle invited him to come and coach at Taylor. "I [Davenport] didn't know anything about coaching."[26] At the time he was 24 years old, and had been a professional football player in Canada since graduating from college. Odle was persuasive and Davenport came to Taylor for spring training in 1957. Odle was determined to find a football coach who would transform the Taylor football program and take Taylor to a new level of recognition. According to Davenport, "Coach" had a vision for the future of sports at Taylor where "a lot more was going to happen... Don's a very bright guy, a show boater who saw pzzazz or splash as the way to get rid of the fuddy duddy image Taylor had at the time.... He had a

pretty serious agenda."[27] Odle's agenda was attractive
to Davenport and he entered into it whole heartedly.

When Davenport came for the 1957 spring training Odle asked another professor and his wife to meet
him at the airport instructing them to "bring him
[Davenport] in the back way so he wouldn't see how
small Upland was." Odle arranged for Davenport to
meet Dr. Milo Rediger, the Academic Dean, who told
him, "you are an all-American. That is as good as an
M.A. to me."[28] Davenport agreed to come and to coach
for one year even though this meant uprooting his
family. Bob and Barbara Ballard Davenport arrived
in Upland with their two young children in the fall of
1958. The transition from the West Coast to a small
Indiana town was especially difficult for Barbara. She
"cried when she had to give up her California license
plate." Before the Davenports built their own home,
during the first year they lived in the "shacks", hastily
constructed barracks built after World War II to house
returning servicemen.[29]

During Davenport's first two years the Taylor football team's record was not particularly good. He said
that if he did not win at least eight games during the
third season he would leave. His team did win eight
contests, losing one and earning Taylor's first conference title in football. Subsequently, he delivered four
more conference championships during his tenure as
coach. Davenport followed Odle's practice of encouraging his athletes, dressed sharply in matching blaz-
ers and ties, to speak and sing at local churches and
other meetings such as Youth for Christ rallies.[30]

Odle encouraged Davenport to become involved in
a speaking routine similar to his own. At one point
Davenport was addressing groups four and five times
a week, driving some 50,000 miles a year. One night
while he was driving home Davenport recalls he had
an unusual spiritual experience. He believes he heard
an audible voice in the car saying, "Give me your
summer."[31] In response, in the summer of 1964 he
took a group of football players on a bicycle trip along
the Mississippi River. He had no intention of continu-

ing these trips. However he was persuaded the following summer to lead a one thousand mile bicycle tour which would prove to be the beginning of a successful program.

The philosophy of Wandering Wheels is stated in the organization's brochure:

> Originally, the program was aimed at providing church youth with a program of adventure and physical challenge. Wheels wanted to help church youth to develop pride in good things that come from attending church and growing in Christ's teachings. Over the years a balance of serving youth and adults has evolved. The program has grown to embrace all church denominations and non-church related programs.... It is Wheels' desire to associate its activities with the local church, to celebrate the church. Wheels feels the participants encourage the local congregation by bringing the excitement of their travels into the church.[32]

Coach Davenport

One of the hallmarks of Wheels has been long distance bicycle touring. In 1966 Wheels sponsored a 3000 mile coast to coast bicycle trip in which between 70 and 80% of the participants were Taylor students. This expanded through the decades so that by 1994 over 40 coast to coast tours were completed involving hundreds of riders, both male and female, ranging in ages from 12 to 74. By 1969, Wheels had grown from a three month summer to a year around program. In both 1985 and 1987 "Circle America" tours were com-

The Power of Many

pleted with one hundred cyclists participating in the two 10,000 mile circuits. Wheels developed a number of safety features for bicycles which now are known throughout the nation. These include a bicycle safety flag (1966), hardshell helmets (1967), bright easily seen riding accessories (1970), and special mirrors (1980). Several movies have also been produced featuring the program and it has been the subject of a vari-

Coast-to-coast with Chinese friends

ety of media documentaries and articles.[33] During the Lyndon Johnson administration a Wheels group was welcomed at the White House.

The program was growing so rapidly and showing such great promise that Davenport decided in 1968 to resign from his football responsibilities at Taylor in order to devote full time to his organization. Initially, he maintained his relationship with Taylor University by reporting to the Development Office, and later directly to the Office of the President.

In the late sixties and early seventies Davenport created tours to Europe and to Israel, the latter connected to a Bible Literature course taught by Taylor's Religion Department which became a regular feature of the Wheels program. At this time Taylor University did not have a strong overseas study program, and Wheels was one of the first concerted efforts to encourage students and faculty to travel abroad with an academic component. In the fall of 1987 Wheels sponsored a January tour to the People's Republic of China. The opportunity to earn academic credit for a course entitled History of Modern China taught by Professor Alan Winquist was a part of this experience. The following year Wheels hosted and funded thirty cyclists from China in a coast to coast tour under its leadership. Wheels has also sponsored tours to Russia and Alaska. The Wheels concept gave birth to at least fifty other Christian bicycle groups though none of them have lasted over a long period of time as has Wheels.[34] Wandering Wheels truly has been a unique part of sports evangelism.

The vision of sports evangelism born in the minds of Hillis and Culver and implemented by Odle has evolved and expanded as many people have seized the opportunity to connect their interest in athletics with their understanding of the Christian imperative to spread the Gospel across the globe. One man's willingness to risk reputation and resources and step out in faith has inspired many other Christians to put legs on their own dreams. Venture for Victory was the beginning. Organizations such as Friendship Sports and Wandering Wheels carry on the mission, and undoubtedly others will follow.

CONCLUSION

It is appropriate to raise two questions at the conclusion of this book. First how does one evaluate the overall significance of Venture for Victory? Secondly how does one measure the impact of Don Odle?

An important characteristic of the contemporary era is the extraordinary influence of athletics and athletes on the lives of people around the globe. This is a "sports crazed" generation and the church is effectively capitalizing on this phenomenon. Eddie Waxer, a founder of Pro Athletes Outreach (1971) and a leader in the 1986 formation of the International Sports Coalition (ISC) likens the current worldwide sports ministry programs to "an explosion which has happened in our midst."[1] He has visited most of the world's nations, and estimates there are currently at least some 400 sports ministry programs around the

213

globe with additional programs being supported by local congregations. In the words of Jack King, "sports evangelism has become a mega movement."[2]

According to Waxer, Christians outside the United States recognize the importance of Venture for Victory as the beginning of sports evangelism. These hundreds of sports ministry programs can trace their lineage back to VV; it is the model used throughout the world.[3] One example is Great Britain's Christians in Sport organization. Its current director, Reverend Andrew Wingfield-Digby credits VV as the model for this successful ministry organization.[4]

Waxer describes VV as a "cutting edge ministry focusing on faith, created long before its time." In his view "the Spirit of God chose to birth this real modern day pioneering ministry as a church planting mission movement rather than a fellowship of Christian athletes."[5] VV's goal from the outset was to recruit a number of committed Christian college age basketball players to set aside either the entire summer or part of a summer for the specific purpose of playing games overseas and more importantly to preach the Gospel at half times as well as in local churches on Sundays. After the games, the team would remain to interact with the fans and to help distribute Christian literature. The VV model required a close working relationship with local missionaries. They presented the players to the fans, resulting in the missionaries becoming more visible locally and nationally. The missionaries followed up on the spectators who had made decisions for Christ. This cooperative relationship led to significant expansion of the Christian church in the countries visited by the VV teams. One of the career missionaries involved with VV from the early days was Charles (Chuck) Holsinger. He noted that at one time one out of every sixty people in Taiwan were enrolled in a Bible correspondence course, a direct outgrowth of the VV games. Missionaries connected with several different organizations including OMS, OC and the Navigators worked together to encourage people in some 6,000 villages in Taiwan to enroll in

Conclusion

these courses. These organizations also distributed one million copies of the Gospel of John in Chinese. As a result there was an impressive increase in church membership; the Presbyterian Church in Taiwan, for example, more than doubled in size.[6]

A second major way in which VV exerted influence can be observed in the lives of numerous athletes who played on VV teams. Many players including Bud Schaeffer, Don Granitz, Clyde Cook, and Norm Cook were inspired in large part to become career missionaries as a result of their involvement with VV. Others established a life long fascination for and interest in the countries they visited. Tim Diller was one such player whose life was shaped by the VV experience. He recalls that Odle encouraged his players to develop a world view. Diller was especially impressed by the generosity and dedication of the missionaries he met. After graduating from Taylor University, Diller attended Fuller Seminary in anticipation of returning to the Philippines as a Wycliffe Bible translator. After his seminary studies, from 1965 to 1968 he attended UCLA, receiving an MA and Ph.D in linguistics. His doctoral dissertation was a grammar of the Waray language spoken on the island of Leyte in the Philippines. He and his wife, Lucy, and their first child spent a year in the Philippines gathering material for the dissertation and traveling extensively. Though the Dillers ultimately decided not to pursue their initial goal of working with Wycliffe, they maintained relationships with many of the missionaries they met in those early days. As a result, three of the Diller's four children are involved in some way with world wide missions.[7]

Many coaches and leaders of current evangelistic sports teams developed their vision of ministry through their connection with VV, later integrated into OC as Sports Ambassadors (SA). An example of one such leader is Don Callan who has spent a number of years coaching and teaching at Cedarville College in Ohio where he directs a highly successful sports evangelism program. In 1960 he founded the Missionary Internship Service in conjunction with the campus pastor. During the summer of 1968 and 1969 he traveled with Sports Ambassadors teams, coaching and giving basketball clinics. He has personally made over twenty tours through Asia with Cedarville basketball, track, and soccer teams. After twenty-five years of traveling to the Philippines, Mongolia, and Nepal, Callan added Madrid, Spain to his summer schedule.[8] In 1984 Chuck Holsinger and Bud Schaeffer were invited to come to the Olympic Village in Colorado Springs to talk about evangelistic sports teams. There were 33 coaches from across the United States at this meeting and 29 of them had played on VV/SA teams.

Finally, VV/SA had a significant impact on the founding of other important sports evangelistic ministries, most notably Athletes in Action (AIA) and the Fellowship of Christian Athletes (FCA). The former organization is a part of Campus Crusade for Christ founded by Bill Bright at UCLA in 1951. AIA had its official beginnings in 1966. It combines the two goals of reaching specific athletes and through them of evangelizing the spectators at sporting events. FCA was founded in 1954 by Don McClannen, a basketball coach at Eastern Oklahoma A&M.[9] Its focus is on athletes and is active on hundreds of high school and college campuses across the United States. Many other groups focusing on either mass evangelism through sports or working with athletes have emerged from these two pioneering groups. Waxer believes that there are currently at least 25,000 professional athletes worldwide who profess to "know Christ."[10]

What has been Coach Odle's impact? Ironically, outside of the United States and East Asia, many people would not recognize the name Don Odle or Taylor University in connection with the birthing of the sports evangelistic movement. However, virtually everyone interviewed by the authors of this study stated that Don Odle should be given credit for being "the father of sports evangelism" in our era. Holsinger, for example, identified Odle's decision to bring his basketball team to Taiwan in 1952 as the key to OC's subsequent success in evangelizing several East

Conclusion

Asian countries. "If he had not responded we would never have had the first and second VV teams. These teams opened the Philippines, Vietnam, Japan and Korea to OCI [OC]"[11]

OC was not the only organization to benefit from the VV experiences. Taylor University also reaped the rewards of this innovative venture. George Glass whose life was deeply impacted by his involvement with Odle notes that VV placed Taylor "light years ahead" of other schools because there were no other programs like it at the time.[12] Odle was a charismatic speaker who was much in demand. He spoke to countless groups about the VV experience, always emphasizing Taylor University wherever he spoke.

Of course if Odle had not already established a successful athletic program at Taylor University he would not have had a basketball team worthy of the high level of international competition that was encountered in East Asia. According to George Glass, Odle was the man who brought Taylor University into the athletic world. Prior to Odle's coming to Taylor the athletic program was almost "non-existent"; it was on a "Sunday School level—really embarrassing."[13] Odle "broke the mold" by developing innovative approaches and introducing new levels of athletic competition. More importantly, Odle brought a special emotional energy to the teams he coached. For example, Glass remembers that the basketball team of which he was a member rarely lost a game when they played on Taylor's home court.[14] Jack King stated that while Odle was probably not technically the greatest coach, his enthusiasm for the game and his commitment to his players enabled him to be a "great motivator." Tim Diller recalled that even though "Coach" demanded a lot from his players they were willing to deliver. "We worked very hard for him!"[15]

There is no question that Odle was a mentor to the athletes who played on his teams. Clyde Cook participated on three VV squads and remembers that when Odle called him to inquire if he would go on the 1956 trip, it was "one of the greatest phone calls of my life."

Cook also recalls that during the trip the team ran out of money but Odle located the funds necessary to get them home. What impressed Cook most was Odle's commitment to the Lord and to evangelism. "If you look at the legacy that Don Odle and VV have it is incredible."[16]

Odle's sincere Christian faith is evident to everyone who has been associated with him. Odle is remembered by his players as a "fierce competitor" who wanted to win, but he never lost sight of the real goal—to be an effective Christian witness. For example, Jenkinson stated, "We always knew why we were there... We never, never tried to fool people." Good sportsmanship was taken seriously and when a player occasionally was carried away by a perceived bad call, the team rallied to calm down the situation.[17] Jay Kesler has characterized Odle as having "a pure soul." Odle's main focus has always been his Christian witness. Although he is a "bit of a card" with a strong, competitive personality, he is also very concerned about other people. "I have always been impressed by this aspect of Odle's life," noted Taylor University's former President.[18]

Odle was a spiritual mentor to his players. Larry Winterholter was one of those athletes who came to Taylor prior to having made a Christian commitment. It was largely due to Coach Odle's efforts that Winterholter became interested in the Christian Gospel. He recalls that "Coach" was "on his trail constantly" causing him to try to avoid Odle except at practice. However, in his junior year as a result of regular spiritual discipling from Odle, he made a profession of faith.[19] Glass declared that Odle touched every significant aspect of his life including his spiritual development. He recalls the very date - October 14, 1955 - when Odle called him into his office and "opened the word of God." As a result of this experience Glass committed himself to Christ and "life took on a different perspective. Taylor University became my home and my church."[20] Roger Jenkinson stated, Odle's Christian commitment was "unwavering". Even

Conclusion

though he was not a theologian his message was simple and "right on target."[21]

In a special Taylor chapel honoring VV players held on September 22, 1995, Norm Cook commented that Odle's impact was "absolutely phenomenal—he set the standard for us."[22] Odle was totally dedicated to the VV program recruiting high caliber players year after year, raising the necessary funds to support the program, telling the VV story in many places to many people, and traveling with the teams to East Asia and South America.

The story of modern Christian sports evangelism began with a simple phone call in February 1952. Despite almost insurmountable obstacles, Don Odle successfully displayed "the power of one" by seizing the opportunity to bring a Christian basketball team to East Asia during the summer of 1952. From that humble beginning, Venture for Victory's fame gradually spread during the next decade. "The power of one" was transformed into "the power of the many". As former VV basketball star Forrest Jackson has observed, "Don Odle cast a vision which others followed."[23]

Coach Odle has served the Church well in developing new strategies to reach people who would not normally respond to the traditional methods of evangelism. Odle's life truly exhibits a "full court press" in furthering Christ's message on earth.

Endnotes

Chapter One Notes

[1] Don Odle, *Taylor Made*, unpublished manuscript, p. 5.

[2] Don Odle, *Taylor Made*, p. 5.

[3] Don Odle, *Taylor Made*, p. 5.

[4] Don Odle, interview by authors, Muncie, Indiana, 9 October 2000.

[5] Don Odle, *Taylor Made*, p. 10.

[6] Don Odle, *Taylor Made*, p. 10.

[7] Don Odle, *Taylor Made*, p. 11.

[8] Don Odle, *Taylor Made*, p. 2.

[9] Don Odle, interview by authors, Oldsmar, Florida, 6 February 1999.

[10] Don Odle, *Taylor Made*, p. 4.

[11] Don Odle, *Taylor Made*, p. 2.

[12] Don Odle, *Taylor Made*, p. 2.

[13] Don Odle, *Taylor Made*, p. 8.

[14] Don Odle, *Taylor Made*, p. 2.

[15] Don Odle, *Taylor Made*, p. 6.

[16] Don Odle, *Taylor Made*, p. 6.

[17] Don Odle, *Taylor Made*, p. 6.

[18] Don Odle, *Taylor Made*, p. 7.

[19] Don Odle, *Taylor Made*, p. 9.

[20] Don Odle, *Taylor Made*, p. 10.

[21] Josephine Erler Miller, interview by authors, Upland, Indiana, 22 July 2000.

[22] Don Odle. *Taylor Made*, p. 10.

[23] Don Odle, *Taylor Made*, p. 9.

[24] Don Odle, *Taylor Made*, p. 11.

[25] Odle's concern about his lack of height stayed with him throughout his career. Many years later, he and Bonnie had a tombstone designed with the inscription "He never Dunked!" This is what Odle says is his "only regret."

Endnotes

[26] *The Gem*. 1939, p. 91.

[27] William Ringenberg, *Taylor University The First 150 Years* (Upland: Taylor University Press, 1996), p. 130.

[28] *The Gem*, 1935, 1936, 1937.

[29] *The Gem*, 1940, p. 87.

[30] *The Gem*, 1941, p. 104.

[31] *The Gem*, 1941, p. 78.

[32] *The Gem*, 1941, p. 102.

[33] Don Odle, *Taylor Made*, p. 25.

[34] Bonnie Odle, interview by authors, Muncie, Indiana, 2 September, 2000.

[35] Bonnie Odle, interview by authors, Muncie, Indiana, 2 September, 2000.

[36] Bonnie Odle, interview by authors, Muncie, Indiana, 2 September, 2000.

[37] Bonnie Odle, interview by authors, Muncie, Indiana, 2 September, 2000.

[38] Bonnie Odle, interview by authors, Muncie, Indiana, 2 September, 2000.

[39] Don Odle, *Taylor Made*, p. 25.

[40] Don Odle, *Taylor Made*, p. 25.

[41] Bonnie Odle, interview by authors, Muncie, Indiana, 2 September, 2000.

[42] Don Odle, interview by authors, Muncie, Indiana, 2 September, 2000.

[43] Don Odle, *Taylor Made*, p. 28.

[44] Program for the Annual Alumni Celebration, Union Township Schools, 20 May, 2000.

[45] Don Odle, *Taylor Made*, p. 33.

[46] Don Odle, *Taylor Made*, pp. 33, 34.

[47] Don Odle, *Taylor Made*, p. 34.

[48] *The Anderson Herald*, Dec 1943 as quoted in Don Odle, *Taylor Made*, p. 35.

[49] Don Odle, *Taylor Made*, p. 43.

[50] Don Odle, *Taylor Made*, p. 37.

[51] Don Odle, *Taylor Made*, p. 38.

[52] Don Odle, *Taylor Made*, p. 104.

[53] Don Odle, *Taylor Made*, p. 103.

[54] Don Odle, *Taylor Made*, p. 104.

[55] Don Odle, *Taylor Made*, p. 105.

[56] Don Odle, *Taylor Made*, p. 105.

[57] Don Odle, *Taylor Made*, p. 47.

[58] *The Gem*. 1949, p. 104.

[59] Don Odle, *Taylor Made*, p. 52.

[60] Don Odle, *Taylor Made*, p. 48.

[61] *The Gem*, 1950, pp. 75, 78.

[62] *The Gem*, 1948, p. 10

[63] *The Gem*, 1949, p. 106.

[64] *The Gem*, 1950, p. 80.

[65] Don Odle, *Taylor Made*, p. 61.

[66] Ted Wright, interview by authors, Upland, Indiana, 12 February 2001.

[67] Ted Wright, interview by authors, Upland, Indiana, 12 February 2001.

[68] Don Odle, *Taylor Made*, p. 62.

[69] Don Odle, *Taylor Made*, p. 62.

[70] *The Binghamton Press*, 27 December 1950.

[71] Ted Wright, interview by authors in Upland, Indiana, 12 February 2001.

[72] Don Odle, *Taylor Made*, p. 63.

[73] Ted Wright, interview by authors, Upland, Indiana, 12 February 2001.

[74] *The Gem*, 1951, p. 86.

[75] The losses were to Concordia of St. Louis, Franklin, twice to Indiana Central, St Michaels, Wheaton, and Evansville. *The Gem*, 1951, p. 86.

[76] *The Gem*, 1951, p. 86.

[77] *The Gem*, 1951, p. 87.

[78] *The Gem*, 1952, p. 106.

[79] *The Gem*, 1953, pp. 98, 99.

[80] *The Gem*, 1953, p. 101.

[81] *The Gem*, 1955, p. 98.

[82] *The Gem*, 1949, p. 112.

[83] *The Gem*, 1951, p. 88.

[84] *The Gem*, 1952, p. 110.

[85] Don Odle, *Taylor Made*, p. 116.

[86] Don Odle, *Taylor Made*, p. 118.

[87] Don Odle, *Taylor Made*, p. 118.

[88] Don Odle, *Taylor Made*, p. 117.

[89] Don Odle, *Taylor Made*, p. 209.

[90] Don Odle, *Taylor Made*, p. 117.

[91] *The Echo*, 22 February 1955.

[92] *The Echo*, 22 February 1955.

Chapter Two Notes

[1] Jan Winebrenner, *Steel in His Soul, The Dick Hillis Story* (Mulkiteo, WA: WinePress Publishing, 1996) pp. 42-44.

[2] Winebrenner, *Steel in His Soul*, pp. 71, 77.

[3] Winebrenner, *Steel in His Soul*, p. 79.

[4] Winebrenner, *Steel in His Soul*, p. 92.

[5] Winebrenner, *Steel in His Soul*, p. 92.

Endnotes

[6] Jonathan Spence, *The Search for Modern China* (New York: Norton, 1990), p. 382.

[7] Don Odle, *Venture for Victory (Berne, Indiana: Light and Hope Publications, 1954)*, p. 146.

[8] Winebrenner, *Steel in His Soul*, p. 152.

[9] John Pollock, *Billy Graham, the Authorized Biography* (New York: McGraw Hill, 1966), p. 31.

[10] Pollock, *Billy Graham*, p. 32.

[11] Pollock, *Billy Graham*, p. 31.

[12] Pollock, *Billy Graham*, p. 32.

[13] Pollock, *Billy Graham*, p. 33.

[14] Marilee Pierce Dunker, *Man of Vision Woman of Prayer* (Nashville, Tennessee: T. Nelson, 1980), p. 74.

[15] Dunker, *Man of Vision Woman of Prayer*, p. 89.

[16] Dunker, *Man of Vision Woman of Prayer*, p. 101.

[17] Winebrenner, *Steel in His Soul*, pp. 147, 148.

[18] Winebrenner, *Steel in His Soul*, pp. 147, 148.

[19] Winebrenner, *Steel in His Soul*, p. 149.

[20] Winebrenner, *Steel in His Soul*, p. 150.

[21] Winebrenner, *Steel in His Soul*, p. 152.

[22] Muriel Cook Culver interview by authors, Upland, Indiana, 17 July 2000.

[23] Winebrenner, *Steel in His Soul*, p. 158.

[24] Winebrenner, *Steel in His Soul*, p. 159.

[25] Winebrenner, *Steel in His Soul*, p. 165.

[26] Quoted in Winebrenner, *Steel in His Soul*, p. 165.

[27] Ellsworth Culver, interview by authors, Muncie, Indiana, 29 June 2001. Culver remained with Orient Crusades until 1958 when he joined World Vision as Executive Vice President and led the organization's expansion throughout Asia and Latin America. During the latter part of the 1960s and the first part of the 1970s he worked on inner city social issues in the United States on a variety of programs. In 1970 Culver was appointed Executive Vice President of Food for the Hungry and established the Hunger Corps, providing young adults with opportunities for international volunteer service in community development projects. In 1982 Culver co-founded Mercy Corps, International and directed numerous international relief and development programs in Africa, the Middle East and Central America. Currently he is Senior Vice President of this organizastion providing leadership for new initiatives in North Korea and other parts of East Asia.

[28] Winebrenner, *Steel in His Soul*, pp. 165-167. OC was first incorporated as Gospel Outreach but the name Formosa Gospel Crusades was widely used. In 1952 it became Orient Crusades in order to more accurately reflect its expanded work to the Philippines. A major factor in this expansion was a challenge issued to Hillis by Billy Graham. "The Philippines needs you... The country is ripe for the kind of work you are doing. Would you consider sending a team there, too?" (Graham quoted in Winebrenner, *Steel in His Soul*, p. 194). Later in the 1950s Orient Crusades expanded into Hong Kong, Okinawa, South Korea, and South Vietnam. In 1956 Hillis was approached by a missionary to consider work in Argentina. Because of its expansion beyond East Asia, the name was changed in 1958 to Overseas Crusades. By 1981 OC International had expanded into nine additional countries in East Asia, Latin America, and Europe as well as Australia. Currently the ministry of OC International has expanded into 22 countries on five continents. The mission cooperated in establishing Morrison Academy in Taiwan and Faith Academy in the Philippines, two schools serving primarily sons and daughters of missionaries. Hillis was the General Director from its founding until 1971. In 1962 he moved to California to be at the mission's headquarters in Palo Alto. After 1971 Hillis continued to travel to various OC fields where he supported the missionary efforts.

[29] Winebrenner, *Steel in His Soul,* p. 187.

[30] Ellsworth Culver, interview by authors, Muncie, Indiana, 29 June 2001.

[31] Winebrenner, *Steel in His Soul,* p. 190.

[32] Ellsworth Culver, interview by authors, Muncie, Indiana, 29 June 2001.

[33] Ted Engstrom, telephone interview by authors, Upland, Indiana, 3 March 2000.

[34] The early presidents of YFC/USA were: Torrey Johnson 1945-48; Bob Cook 1948-57; Ted Engstrom 1957-63; Carl Bihl 1963-65; Samuel Wolgemuth 1965-73; Jay Kesler 1973-85). Engstrom, Wolgemuth and Kesler are Taylor University alumni. Engstrom remained with YFC until 1963 when Dr. Bob Pierce invited him to take a position as Executive Vice President with World Vision. Eventually Engstrom became President of this organization (currently he is its President Emeritus). He has authored 52 books. Odle has commented that "if Taylor athletics were to name its biggest encourager and role model, it would be Ted Engstrom. For over 60 years, he has been a close friend and inspiration to Taylor's people." (Odle interview 2-5-99) In 1996, Engstrom was inducted into the Taylor University Athletic Hall of Fame. The citation reads: 1938. "A Man With a Vision" four year letterman in baseball – played semi-pro Member, chairman of the Board of the Trustees [Taylor University], 1948-61.

Endnotes

Key to the expansion of the Athletic Department. Directed the contacts and support for the Venture for Victory program. President—Youth for Christ, publisher of Campus Life Magazine. President Emeritus—World Vision International. A prolific editor and author. Key—"Managing Your Time" and "The Meaning of a Christian Leader." He has not only challenged others toward excellence in thought, word and deed; He has, first of all, required excellence of himself. Thank you, Ted!

Chapter Three Notes

[1] Don Odle, interview by authors, Oldsmar, Florida, 6 February 1999.

[2] Don Odle, interview by authors, Oldsmar, Florida, 6 February 1999.

[3] Don Odle, interview by authors, Oldsmar, Florida, 6 February 1999.

[4] Don Odle, interview by authors, Oldsmar, Florida, 6 February 1999.

[5] Don Odle, interview by authors, Oldsmar, Florida, 6 February 1999.

[6] Don Odle, interview by authors, Oldsmar, Florida, 6 February 1999.

[7] Don Granitz scrapbook, clipping from *The Echo*.

[8] Taylor University Chapel, Don Odle's comments, 22 September 1995.

[9] Don Granitz, interview by authors, Upland, Indiana, 15 March 2000.

[10] Don Granitz, interview by authors, Upland, Indiana, 15 March 2000.

[11] Taylor University Chapel, Don Odle's comments, 22 September 1995.

[12] Taylor University Chapel, Don Odle's comments, 22 September 1995.

[13] Taylor University Chapel, Don Odle's comments. 22 September 1995.

[14] *The Gem*, 1953, 96.

[15] *The Gem*, 1954, 90.

[16] *The Echo*, 11/23/54.

[17] Odle, *Venture for Victory*, p. 30.

[18] Norm Cook, interview by authors, Winona Lake, Indiana, 8 July 2000.

[19] Bud Schaeffer, telephone interview by authors, Upland, Indiana, 6 July 2000.

[20] Don Odle, interview by authors, Oldsmar, Florida, 6 February 1999.

[21] Odle. *Venture for Victory*, p. 18.

[22] Odle. *Venture for Victory*, p. 18.

[23] Odle. *Venture for Victory*, p. 23.

[24] Don Odle, interview by authors, Oldsmar, Florida, 6 February 1999.

[25] Quoted in *The Echo*. April 1, 1952.

[26] Don Odle, interview by authors, Olsdmar, Florida, 6 February 1999.

[27] Odle, *Venture for Victory*, p. 24.

[28] *The Echo*. April 1, 1952.

[29] Don Granitz scrapbook, newspaper clipping.

[30] Don Granitz scrapbook, newspaper clipping.

[31] Don Odle, interview by authors, Oldsmar, Florida, 6 February 1999.

[32] Granitz scrapbook.

[33] Odle, *Venture for Victory*, p. 28.

[34] *Manila Times*, 5/31/52, p. 8.

[35] Don Granitz scrapbook, *Manila Herald* photo.

[36] *The Manila Times*. 6/1/52.

[37] Don Granitz scrapbook. Manila newspaper clipping.

[38] *Manila Times*, 6/3/52, p. 8.

[39] Don Granitz scrapbook, newspaper clipping.

[40] Odle, *Venture for Victory*, p. 28.

[41] Odle, *Venture for Victory*, pp. 151-52.

[42] Odle, *Venture for Victory*, pp. 137-38

[43] Norm and Muriel Cook, interview by authors, Upland, Indiana, 17 July 2000.

[44] Odle, *Venture for Victory*, p. 64.

[45] Odle, *Venture for Victory*, p. 61.

[46] Odle, *Venture for Victory*, p. 61.

[47] Don Granitz scrapbook, newspaper clipping.

[48] Odle, *Venture for Victory*, p. 62.

[49] Odle, *Venture for Victory*, p. 63.

[50] Don Odle, interview by authors, Oldsmar, Florida, 6 February 1999.

[51] Odle. *Taylor Made*. p. 166.

[52] Odle, *Venture for Victory*, p. 64.

[53] Odle, *Venture for Victory*, p. 66.

[54] *Manila Times*, 8/12/52, p. 6.

[55] *Manila Times*, 8/13/52, p. 8.

[56] *Manila Times*, 8/14/52, p. 9.

[57] *Manila Times*, 8/16/52, p .9.

[58] Don Odle, interview by authors, Oldsmar, Florida, 6 February 1999.

Chapter Four Notes

[1] Kenneth Lee Wilson, *Angel At Her Shoulder: Lillian Dickson and Her Taiwan Mission* (New York: Harper & Row, 1964), pp. 134, 135.

[2] Wilson, *Angel At Her Shoulder*, p. 137.

[3] Wilson, *Angel At Her Shoulder*, p. 142.

Endnotes

[4] Odle, Venture for Victory, pp. 99, 100.

[5] Taylor University chapel service, 22 September, 1995.

[6] Wilson, *Angel At Her Shoulder*, p. 169.

> *The Christian Herald* began publication in 1894 when its main mission was to call attention to the suffering among the poor of New York City. They purchased the Bowery Mission and extended their ministry internationally by collecting food and other necessities, and distributing them using their "mercy fleets." They also established eleven orphanages in China, Hong Kong, and Korea. At one point 1400 children were being served in these institutions.

[7] Wilson, *Angel At Her Shoulder*, p. 171.

[8] Charles P. Culver had been a student at Taylor university in 1915 and was a member of the Thalonian Society basketball team.

[9] When Norm and Muriel Cook returned to China years later, they went to Fuzhow and met the pastor of the Flowergate Church. He told them that he had been one of her father's orphan boys and that her father had arranged his marriage for him. Many of the boys who were rescued by Culver had become pastors.

[10] Muriel Cook, interview by authors, Upland, Indiana, 17 July 2000.

[11] Norm Cook, interview by authors, Winona Lake, Indiana, 8 July 2000.

[12] Norm Cook, interview by authors, Winona Lake, Indiana, 8 July 2000.

[13] Norm Cook, interview by authors, Winona Lake, Indiana, 8 July 2000.

[14] Norm and Muriel Cook, interview by authors, Upland, Indiana, 17 July 2000.

[15] Norm and Muriel Cook, interview by authors, Upland, Indiana, 17 July 2000.

[16] Norm and Muriel Cook, interview by authors, Upland, Indiana, 17 July 2000.

[17] Norm Cook, interview by authors, Winona Lake, Indiana, 8 July 2000.

[18] Norm and Muriel Cook, interview by authors, Upland, Indiana, 17 July 2000.

[21] Norm and Muriel Cook, interview by authors, Upland, Indiana, 17 July 2000.

[19] Taylor University, chapel service, 22 September 1995.

[20] Norm Cook, interview by authors, Winona Lake, Indiana, 8 July 2000.

[22] Don Odle, *Venture for Victory*, pp. 56-57.

[24] Don Odle, *Venture for Victory*, pp. 94-96.

[23] Taylor University, chapel service, 22 September 1995.

[25] Norm and Muriel Cook, interview by authors, Upland, Indiana, 17 July 2000.

[26] Norm Cook, interview by authors, Winona Lake, Indiana, 8 July 2000.

[27] Roger Jenkinson, interview by authors, Upland, Indiana, 1 May 2000.

[28] Biographical information in Charles Holsinger, *Above the Cry of Battle.* Antipolo City, Philippines: Missionary Training Center, 2000.

[29] Holsinger, Above the Cry of Battle, p. 37.

[30] In January 1945 Holsinger's unit met Japanese resistance in the battle of Lupao.
"The 25th Infantry Division saw more combat in the Philippines than did any other. And Chuck was smack dab in the middle of it. His God-given leadership ability and courage earned him a Silver Star for gallantry in action." (quote by Lloyd O. Cory, retired soldier, World War II, back cover of Holsinger, *Above the Cry of Battle*) The citation (25 June 1945) for the silver star read in part that "[His] gallant actions in the face of grave danger, which limited the enemy's infiltration and enabled his platoon to hold its ground, were in keeping with the highest traditions of the military service." (quoted in Appendix, *Above the Cry of Battle*, p. 249)

[31] Holsinger, *Above the Cry of Battle*, p. 247.

[32] Chuck Holsinger, interview by authors, Upland, Indiana, 11 July 2000.

[33] Chuck Holsinger, interview by authors, Upland, Indiana, 11 July 2000.

[34] Janet Holsinger Friesen, interview by authors, Upland, Indiana, 29 July 2000.

[35] Bud Schaeffer, telephone interview by authors, Upland, Indiana, 6 July 2000.

Chapter Five Notes

[1] Don Jacobsen's Diary describing the 1953 VV tour was an invaluable source in writing this chapter.

[2] Don Jacobsen, interview by authors, Upland, Indiana, 24 May 2000.
Since 1974, Jacobsen has been a member of the Taylor University Board of Trustees and was instrumental in revitalizing the William Taylor Foundation. He has had a successful management career at AT & T and has been Executive Director of Ravi Zacharias International ministries headquarted in Atlanta, Georgia.

[3] Don Odle, interview by authors, Oldsmar, Florida, 6 February 1999.

[4] Don and Bonnie Odle, interview by authors, Oldsmar, Florida, 6 February 1999.

[5] Don Jacobsen, unpublished Diary, 18 June 1953.

Endnotes

[6] *Manila Times,* 19 June 1953.

[7] Jacobsen, Diary, 19 June 1953.

[8] Jacobsen, Diary, 20 June 1953 and 22 June 1953.

[9] Jacobsen, Diary, 21 June 1953.

[10] Jacobsen, Diary, 22 June 1953 and 29 June 1953.

[11] Jacobsen, Diary, 21 June 1953.

[12] Jacobsen, Diary, 4 July 1953.

[13] Jacobsen, Diary, 8 July 1953.

[14] *Manila Times,* 19 June 1953.

[15] Jacobsen, Diary, 20 June 1953.

[16] Jacobsen, Diary, 24 June 1953.

[17] Jacobsen, Diary, 26 June 1953.

[18] Jacobsen, Diary, 26 June 1953.

[19] Jacobsen, Diary, 17 July 1953.

[20] *China News,* 18 July 1953.

[21] Jacobsen, Diary, 18 July 1953.

[22] *China News,* July 23 1953.

[23] Jacobsen, Diary, 24 July 1953.

[24] *China News,* 25 July 1953.

[25] *China News,* 26 July 1953.

[26] Jacobsen, Diary. 21 July, 1953.

[27] Jacobsen, Diary, 21 July 1953.

[28] Jacobsen, Diary, 7 August 1953.

[29] Jacobsen. Diary, 24 July 1953.

[30] Jacobsen, Diary, 22 July 1953.

[31] Jacobsen, Diary, 26 and 27 July 1953.

[32] Jacobsen, Diary, 28 and 29 July 1953.

[33] Jacobsen, Diary, 30 July 1953.

[34] Jacobsen, Diary, 28 July and 1 August 1953.

[35] Jacobsen, Diary, 10 August 1953.

[36] Clipping from Jacobsen Scrapbook.

[37] Jacobsen, Diary, 11 and 12 August 1953.

[38] Jacobsen, Diary, 11 and 22 August 1953.

[39] Jacobsen, Diary, 15 August 1953.

[40] Don Jacobsen, interview by authors, Upland, Indiana, 24 May 2000.

On June 8, 1957 Lieutenant General Harrison was the commencement speaker at Taylor University. At that time he was U.S. Army commander in the Caribbean area. He was a Baptist lay evangelist. He also became the executive director of the Chicago Evangelical Welfare Agency which was a subsidiary of the National Association of Evangelicals. That agency placed orphaned and deserted children into Christian homes.

[41] Jacobsen, Diary, 24 August 1953.

[42] Jacobsen, Diary, 25 August 1953.

[43] Jacobsen, Diary, 26 August 1953.

[44] Jacobsen, Diary, 27 August 1953.

[45] Jacobsen, Diary, 27 August 1953.

[46] Jacobsen, Diary, 29 August 1953.

[47] Citation. Taylor University Athletic Hall of Fame.

[48] Don Callan, interview by authors, Upland, Indiana, 13 March 2000.

[49] Don Callan, interview by authors, Upland, Indiana, 13 March 2000.

[50] Don Callan, interview by authors, Upland, Indiana, 13 March 2000.

[51] Don Callan, interview by authors, Upland, Indiana, 13 March 2000.

[52] Bud Schaeffer, Letter from Manila, Philippines. July, 1955. Billy Graham Archives, Sports Ambassadors, Collection 132, Box 1.

[53] Bud Schaeffer, Letter, 17 August 1955. Billy Graham Archives, Sports Ambassadors, Collection 132, Box 1.

[54] *Manila Times,* 1 August 1955, p. 13.

[55] *Manila Times,* 2 August 1955, p. 12.

[56] *Manila Times,* 13 August 1955, p. 12.

[57] *Manila Times, 4* August 1955, p. 12.

[58] *Manila Times,* 6 August 1955, p. 12.

[59] *Manila Times,* 6 August 1955, p. 12.

[60] *Manila Times,* 1 August 1955, p. 12.

[61] *Manila Times,* 6 August 1955, p. 13.

[62] *Manila Times*, 23 August 1955, p. 8.

[63] *Manila Times, 23* August 1955, p. 8.

[64] Don Callan, interview by authors, Upland, Indiana, 13 March 2000.

[65] Clyde Cook, telephone interview by authors, Upland, Indiana, 15 March 2001.

[66] Clyde Cook, telephone interview by authors, Upland, Indiana, 15 March 2001.

[67] Don Odle, interview by authors, Muncie, Indiana, 2 October 2000.

[68] Clyde Cook, telephone interview by authors, Upland, Indiana, 15 March 2001.

[69] Clyde Cook, telephone interview by authors, Upland, Indiana, 15 March 2001.

[70] George Glass, interview by authors, Upland, Indiana, 8 March 2000.

[71] George Glass, interview by authors, Upland, Indiana, 8 March 2000.

[72] Jay Kesler, interview by authors, Upland, Indiana, 13 March 2000.

[73] Clyde Cook, telephone interview by authors, Upland, Indiana, 15 March 2001.

Endnotes

[74] Clyde Cook, telephone interview by authors, Upland, Indiana, 15 March 2001.

[75] George Glass, interview by authors, Upland, Indiana, 8 March 2000.

[76] *Manila Times,* 26 July 1957, p. 10.

[77] *Manila Times,* 30 July, 1957, p. 9.

[78] *Manila Times,* 30 July, 1957.

[80] *Manila Times,* 30 July, 1957.

[81] *Manila Times,* 1 August, 1957, p. 8.

[82] *Manila Times,* 10 August, 1957, p. 8.

[83] *Manila Times,* 19 August, 1957, p. 9.

[84] *Manila Times,* 20 August, 1957, p. 8.

[85] *Manila Times,* 16 August, 1957, p. 8.

[86] *Manila Times,* 16 August, 1957, p. 8.

Chapter Six Notes

[1] Odle, *Taylor Made*, p. 150.

[2] Taylor University Athletic Hall of Fame plaque; Roger Jenkinson, interview by authors, Upland, Indiana, 1 May 2000
Jenkinson who is currently professor of geography at Taylor University was born in Cowan, Indiana, near Muncie. As boys, his father and Odle had played against each other in the Muncie leagues. Jenkinson earned majors in math, chemistry and history, but the influence of Professor Grace Olson of the history department and the subsequent impact of the VV experience steered him more and more in the direction of history and geography.

[3] Roger Jenkinson, interview by authors, Upland, Indiana, 1 May 2000.

[4] Roger Jenkinson, interview by authors, Upland, Indiana, 1 May 2000.

[5] *Manila Bulletin,* 14 August 1958.

[6] Roger Jenkinson, interview by authors, Upland, Indiana, 1 May 2000.

[7] *Manila Bulletin,* 14 August 1958.

[8] Bud Schaeffer Prayer Letter, 11 September 1958, Billy Graham Archives, Sports Ambassadors, Collection 132, Box 1.

[9] Roger Jenkinson, interview by authors, Upland, Indiana, 1 May 2000.

[10] Roger Jenkinson, interview by authors, Upland, Indiana, 1 May 2000.

[11] Odle, *Taylor Made*, p. 219
General Chien Ta-Chun was chairman of the Chinese National Olympic Organization. He had been a mayor of Shanghai prior to 1949, and was

a four-star general in Chiang Kai-shek's army in Taiwan. Years later he visited the Taylor University campus, was honored in chapel, and given a banquet in his honor.

[12] Colonel Ho Cha-Pen was the assistant coach and a government official. He was a former Olympic player who had visited Odle in Indiana.

[13] Odle, *Taylor Made*, p. 222.

[14] Odle, *Taylor Made, p. 222.*

[15] Odle, *Taylor Made*, pp. 222-224.

[16] Odle, *Taylor Made*, p. 224.

[17] Odle, *Taylor Made*, p. 224.

[18] Odle, *Taylor Made*, p. 225.

[19] *Manila Times* 18 August 1960, p. 14A.

[20] By August 21 after the arduous nine pre-Olympic tournament days, it became apparent Taiwan was not successful in getting a berth in the final basketball tournament that was to open August 26. The four slots were awarded to Czechoslovakia, Spain, Yugoslavia, and Hungary. The top seeded teams were the United States (defending champion), the USSR, Uruguay, and France. The second seeded teams included Bulgaria, Brazil, the Philippines, and Italy. The Philippines defeated Spain 84-82, but lost to the Poles 86-68 and Uruguay 80-76, thus knocking them out of contention. The other eight teams were Czechoslovakia, Japan, Yugoslavia, Mexico, Poland, Puerto Rico, Spain and Hungary.

[21] Quoted in Odle, *Taylor Made*, p. 228.

[22] Yi-Kuo-Jui. Letter to Odle 17 December 1960. Taylor University has had several other Olympic connections. The first Olympic athlete to attend Taylor was Kuang Ko-yang (Billy Hwang) originally from Hong Kong. He was the Most Valuable Player on the 1960 ROC Olympic basketball team and came to Taylor as a student in 1961. He was a member of the University varsity team in 1961-62. Years later, Eduardo (Ed) Gomez, another Taylor athlete, was a member of the Dominican Republic Olympic basketball team. Sophomore "Go-Go" Gomez amazed fans with his quickness and leaping ability", noted the 1973 *Ilium* (p. 34). Arthur Howard, class of 1934, had taught for years at Lucknow Christian College in India. He developed India's track team and trained the team for the 1960 Olympic games.

Roger Jenkinson, former VV basketball player and former president of the NAIA, was a representative on several Olympic committees. George Glass has served on the Olympics planning committee, judge and official in track and field event in the 1984 Olympics in Los Angeles as well as the Atlanta games in 1996. (continued on page 233)

Endnotes

Coach Odle was instrumental in bringing to Taylor several speakers who were connected with Olympic competition. These included gold medallist Jesse Owens (1936 Olympics), and Witold Zikorski, Poland's 1960 basketball coach.

[23] Norm Nelson is currently professor of missions at George Fox College.

[24] *Manila Times,* 21 and 22 July 1960.

[25] *Manila Times,* 21 July 1960.

[26] Bud Schaeffer Prayer Letter, 15 September 1960. Billy Graham Archives, Sports Ambassadors, Collection 132, Box 1.

[27] *Manila Times* 28 July 1960.

[28] *Manila Times,* 22 July 1960.

[29] *Manila Times,* 27 July 1960.

[30] *Manila Times,* 27 July 1960.

[31] *Manila Times,* 29 July 1960.

[32] *Manila Times,* 30 July 1960.

[33] *Manila Times,* 30 July 1960.

[34] Don Odle, interview by authors, Oldsmar, Florida, 9 February 2000.

[35] Tim Diller, interview by authors, Upland, Indiana, 30 June 2000.

[36] Tim Diller, interview by authors, Upland, Indiana, 30 June 2000.

From 1965 to 1968 Diller went to UCLA, receiving an M.A. and Ph.D in linguistics. He spent a year in the Philippines gathering material for his dissertation. Conditions were sometimes difficult for him and his wife Lucy, and the decision was made not to pursue a missionary life. After returning from the Philippines Diller went to work for a computer firm as a systems analyst. He worked in industry in California and Minnesota before coming to Taylor University in 1981 as a professor in the Computer Science Department.

[37] *Manila Times,* 10 July 1962.

[38] Bud Schaeffer, Prayer Letter, 15 September 1962, Billy Graham Archives, Wheaton, Illinois, Sports Ambassadors, Collection 132, Box 1.

[39] *Manila Times,* 10 July 1962.

[40] *Manila Times,* 10 July 1962.

[41] *Manila Times,* 10 July 1962.

[42] *Manila Times,* 10 July 1962.

[43] *Manila Times,* 11 July 1962.

[44] *Manila Times,* 11 July 1962.

[45] *Manila Times,* 11 July 1962

[46] *Manila Times,* 11 July 1962

[47] *Manila Times,* 11 July 1962.

[48] *Manila Times,* 12 July 1962.

[49] *Manila Times,* 12 July 1962.

[50] *Manila Times,* 13 July 1962.

[51] *Manila Times*, 13 July 1962.

[52] Chris Appel, however, left for Phnom Penh to be involved in the training of the Cambodian basketball team for the 1962 Tokyo Olympics.

[53] Bud Schaeffer Prayer Letter, 15 June 1963, Billy Graham Archives, Sports Ambassadors, Collection 132, Box 1.

[54] *Manila Times,* 3 August 1963.

[55] Bud Schaeffer, Prayer Letter, 15 September 1963, Billy Graham Archives, Sports Ambassadors, Collection 132, Box 1.

[56] Clyde Cook, telephone interview by authors, Upland, Indiana, 14 March 2001.

[57] Clyde Cook, telephone interview by authors, Upland, Indiana, 15 March 2001.

[58] Clyde Cook, telephone interview by authors, Upland, Indiana, 15 March 2001.

[59] *Manila Times,* 3 August 1963.

[60] *Manila Times,* 4 August 1963.

[61] *Manila Times,* 4 August 1963.

[62] *Manila Times,* 6 August 1963.

[63] *Manila Times,* 6 August 1963.

[64] *Manila Times,* 7 August 1963.

[65] *Manila Times,* 7 August 1963.

[66] *Manila Times,* 7 August 1963.

[67] *Manila Times,* 7 August 1963.

[68] Clyde Cook, telephone interview by authors, Upland, Indiana, 15 March 2001.

[69] Antonio Siddayao, "Tall 'N Deadly", *Manila Times,* 26 August 1964.

[70] *Manila Times,* 21 August 1964.

[71] *Manila Times,* 20 August 1964.

[72] *Manila Times,* 2 August 1964.

[73] *Manila Times,* 20 August 1964.

[74] *Manila Times,* 27 August 1964.

[75] *Manila Times,* 21 August 1964.

[76] *Manila Times,* 26 August 1964.

[77] *Manila Times,* 22 August 1964.

[78] *Manila Times,* 23 August 1964.

[79] Antonio Siddayao, "Tall 'N Deadly", *Manila Times,* 24 August 1964.

[80] Antonio Siddayao, "Tall 'N Deadly", *Manila Times,* 24 August 1964.

[81] *Manila Times,* 23 August 1964.

[82] *Manila Times,* 27 August 1964.

[83] *Manila Times,* 27 August 1964.

[84] *Manila Times,* 27 August 1964.

Endnotes

[85] *Manila Times,* 28 August 1964.

[86] *Manila Times,* 28 August 1964.

[87] *Manila Times,* 29 August 1964.

[88] Don Odle, letter to authors 14 September 2000.

[89] Don Odle, interview with authors, Muncie, Indiana, 2 August 2000.

Chapter Seven Notes

[1] Bud Schaeffer, telephone interview by authors, Upland, Indiana, 6 July 2000.

[2] Bud Schaeffer Prayer Letter, October 1968, Billy Graham Archives, Sports Ambassadors, Collection 132, Box 1

[3] Bud Schaeffer letter, August 1969, Billy Graham Archives, Sports Ambassadors, Collection 132, Box 1.

[4] Bud Schaeffer letter, August 1969, Billy Graham Archives, Sports Ambassadors, Collection 132, Box 1.

[5] Jack King, interview by authors, Upland, Indiana, 30 June 2000.

[6] Jack King interview by authors, Upland, Indiana, 30 June 2000.

King was a star athlete at Taylor. When he was inducted into the Taylor Athletic Hall of Fame in 1974, the citation noted that he led the Taylor basketball team to a conference championship in 1959.

[7] Larry Winterholter, interview by authors, Upland, Indiana, 25 July 2000.

[8] Larry Winterholter, interview by authors, Upland, Indiana, 25 July 2000.

[9] Larry Winterholter, interview by authors, Upland, Indiana, 25 July 2000.

[10] Larry Winterholter, interview by authors, Upland, Indiana, 25 July 2000.

[11] Gary Friesen, interview by authors, Upland, Indiana, 12 July 2000.

[12] Gary Friesen, interview by authors, Upland, Indiana, 12 July 2000.

[13] Gary Friesen, interview by authors, Upland, Indiana, 12 July 2000.

[14] Bud Schaeffer letter, 1976, Billy Graham Archives, Sports Ambassadors, Collection 132, Box 1.

[15] Gary Friesen, interview by authors, Upland, Indiana, 12 July 2000.

[16] *The Times* (San Mateo, California), 20 January 1979.

[17] Gary Friesen, interview by authors, Upland, Indiana, 12 July 2000.

[18] Gary Friesen, interview by authors, Upland, Indiana, 12 July 2000.

[19] Odle, *Taylor Made,* 79.

[20] Odle was also inducted into the Indiana Basketball Hall of Fame in 1974.

[21] Odle, *Taylor Made,* unidentified article, p. 248.

[22] Bob Davenport, interview by authors, Upland, Indiana, 3 July 2000.

[23] Barbara Stedman, *Wandering Wheels Coast to Coast* (Upland, Indiana: Wandering Wheels, 1988), 40.

[24] Bob Davenport, interview by authors, Upland, Indiana, 3 July 2000.

[25] Bob Davenport, interview by authors, Upland, Indiana, 3 July 2000.

[26] Bob Davenport, interview by authors, Upland, Indiana, 3 July 2000.

[27] Bob Davenport, interview by authors, Upland, Indiana, 3 July 2000.

[28] Bob Davenport, interview by authors, Upland, Indiana, 3 July 2000.

[29] Barbara Davenport, interview by authors, Upland, Indiana, 6 July 2000. Barbara Davenport is currently employed at Taylor University as Learning Services and Student Athlete Academic Support specialist.

[30] In recognition of Bob Davenport's outstanding contributions, Taylor University honored him in 1973 as a charter member of its Athletic Hall of Fame.

[31] Bob Davenport, interview by authors, Upland, Indiana, 3 July 2000.

[32] *Wandering Wheels Coast to Coast Bicycling Since 1964* (brochure).

[33] *Wandering Wheels Coast to Coast Bicycling Since 1964* (brochure).

[34] Bob Davenport, interview by authors, Upland, Indiana, 3 July 2000.

Conclusion

[1] Eddie Waxer, telephone interview by authors, Upland, Indiana, 28 February 2001.

[2] Jack King, interview by author, Upland, Indiana, 30 June 2000.

[3] Eddie Waxer, telephone interview by authors, Upland, Indiana, 28 February 2001.

[4] Andrew Wingfield-Digby, interview by Alan Winquist, Oxford, United Kingdom, 23 January 2001.

[5] Eddie Waxer, telephone interview by authors, Upland, Indiana, 28 February 2001.

[6] Chuck Holsinger, interview by authors, Upland, Indiana, 11 July 2000.

[7] Tim Diller, interview by authors, Upland, Indiana, 30 June 2000.

[8] Don Callan, telephone interview by authors, Upland, Indiana, 13 March 2000.

[9] Tony Ladd and James A. Mathisen, *Muscular Christianity, Evangelical Protestants and the Development of American Sport* (Grand Rapids, Michigan: Baker Books, 1999), pp. 129-133.

Endnotes

[10] Eddie Waxer, telephone interview by authors, Upland, Indiana, 28 February 2001.

[11] Chuck Holsinger, interview by authors, Upland, Indiana, 11 July 2000.

[12] George Glass, interview by authors, Upland, Indiana, 8 March 2000.

[13] George Glass, interview by authors, Upland, Indiana, 8 March 2000.

[14] George Glass, interview by authors, Upland, Indiana, 8 March 2000.

[15] Tim Diller, interview by authors, Upland, Indiana, 30 June 2000.

[16] Clyde Cook, telephone interview by authors, Upland, Indiana, 15 March 2001.

[17] Roger Jenkinson, interview by authors, Upland, Indiana, 1 May 2000.

[18] Jay Kesler, telephone interview by authors, Upland, Indiana, 12 July 2001.

[19] Larry Winterholter, interview by authors, Upland, Indiana, 25 July 2000.

[20] George Glass, interview by authors, Upland, Indiana, 8 March 2000.

[21] Roger Jenkinson, interview by authors, Upland, Indiana, 1 May 2000.

[22] Taylor University, chapel service, 22 September 1995.

[23] Taylor University, chapel service, 22 September 1995.

About the Authors

The authors with Don and Bonnie Odle

Jessica Rousselow-Winquist is Professor of Communication Arts and Associate Dean for the Division of Fine and Applied Arts at Taylor University. She earned her B.A. at Northwestern College, Minneapolis, and her M.A. and Ph.D. degrees from the University of Minnesota. Her previous research projects have been in the area of rhetorical criticism and women's studies. With her husband, Alan H. Winquist, she co-authored *God's Ordinary People: No Ordinary Heritage* (1996).

Alan H. Winquist has taught at Taylor University since 1973 and is Professor of History. He earned degrees from Wheaton College (Illinois) and Northwestern University before receiving a Ph.D. from New York University in 1976. He has also studied at the University of Stockholm. His books include: *Scandinavians and South Africa: Their Impact on Cultural, Social, and Economic Development before 1900* (1978), and *Swedish-American Landmarks: Where to Go and What to See* (1995).